W9-BZE-395

TABLE OF CONTENTS

INTRODUCTION

The Western world has experienced a revolution. Its consequences are far-reaching; and the sound and fury of this social, political, religious, and moral conflagration grows more deafening with every passing day. Our culture, now almost totally secularized, has repudiated the Judeo-Christian values that have constituted the foundation of our social order for more than 200 years. Revisionism—the practice of writing fiction and calling it history—has become the norm. This repugnant fact is true in education, entertainment, politics, and social life. Revisionists have decided to reinvent the history of the world and, in so doing, have denied the horrors of the Holocaust, stripped virtually every shred of respectability from our national heroes, and celebrated degeneracy with shameless rapacity.

Insatiable appetites for money and trade markets now dictate international policies, often at the expense of national interests and military credibility. Nationalism has given way to the fantasy world of the "global village"—a "village" ready to accept only those willing to be "born again" as merged and muddled, fully secularized humanists.

For some people, such radical changes have mandated a reformatting of evangelical Christianity, particularly in the areas of doctrine and evangelism. They consider doctrine undesirably divisive. Evangelism, in their view, is a gross violation of the new "I'm okay, you're okay," arms-around-the-world camaraderie.

What has come to the contemporary scene is not unfamiliar to us. This kind of ecumenical folly surfaced a few

II PETER

STANDING FAST
IN THE LAST DAYS

by Elwood McQuaid

The Friends of Israel Gospel Ministry, Inc.
P. O. Box 908, Bellmawr, NJ 08099

II PETER: STANDING FAST IN THE LAST DAYS

Elwood McQuaid

Copyright © 2001 by The Friends of Israel Gospel Ministry, Inc.
Bellmawr, NJ 08099

First Printing 2001

Unless otherwise noted, all Scripture is quoted from the *New Scofield Study Bible*, Authorized King James Version, Oxford University Press, Inc., New York, 19670.

Library of Congress Catalog Card Number: 00-132240
ISBN 0-915540-65-7

Cover by Left Coast Design, Portland, OR.

Visit our Web site at *www.foi.org*

generations ago when "enlightened" social-gospel entre-preneurs ravished the mainline denominations. Today just as relentless an attack is being mounted against evangeli-cals who still believe in Jesus' commission to evangelize and conscientiously preserve sound doctrine.

False teachers are blatantly and unashamedly spread-ing their insidious doctrines everywhere. And masses of people who lack discernment and biblical astuteness enthrone these charlatans, then pay homage to them as singular sources of authority worthy of canonization and personal enrichment.

For these reasons, among many others, true believers need the meat and message of the short Epistle of 2 Peter. In the three chapters of his Spirit-directed treatise, the apostle provides all of the essential equipment for dealing with the challenges of living in the last days. Beyond the warnings and admonitions necessary for coping with our demented culture, 2 Peter unveils great vistas of optimism and expectation of what lies ahead for those who know Him. Food for the soul, enlightenment for the mind, and the eternal triumph of the redeemed are all here for the taking, as we fulfill His heart's desire that we "grow in grace, and in the knowledge of our Lord and Savior, Jesus Christ" (2 Pet. 3:18).

emq

A LOOK AT
OURSELVES

Wherefore the rather, brethren, give diligence to make your calling and election sure; for if ye do these things, ye shall never fall. For so an entrance shall be ministered unto you abundantly into the everlasting kingdom of our Lord and Savior, Jesus Christ (2 Pet. 1:10–11).

SIMON PETER   1

*According as his divine power hath given
unto us all things that pertain unto life
and godliness, through the knowledge of
him that hath called us to glory and
virtue; By which are given unto us exceedingly great and precious promises, that by
these ye might be partakers of the divine
nature, having escaped the corruption that
is in the world through lust (1:3-4).*

It is not surprising to hear people talk about our being in
"the last days." Even people who are casually acquainted
with the Scriptures acknowledge that we are living in a
rapidly fragmenting world. As tragedy and trauma develop across the face of our planet, people are trying desper-
ately to make sense of what is happening. What's it all
about? Can we truly create change for the better?

I suppose if we were to select a period of history comparable to our own in political confusion, moral maladjust-
ment, social ineptitude, and individual profligacy, we
could do no better than look to the time of the judges. This
bleak period in the history of ancient Israel tells of a nation

that had lost her way. Fragmented, without unified national leadership, and far removed from her God-given destiny, Israel reeled under attacks from the sword of intruders and the severe rebuke from a God who had better things in mind for these Chosen People. In fact, the defining words of this dismal era were these: "In those days there was no king in Israel; every man did that which was right in his own eyes" (Jud. 21:25).

Thankfully, we have the past to order our conduct and guide our steps into the future. Of all the people who have ever left a footprint on this planet, we have been given the most implements for our betterment—far more, in fact, than any of our forebears. Foremost in our arsenal is the Word of God with all its prophetic and practical revelation. We are a people who can never plead that we were ignorant of the issues or deprived of adequate resources to face the defiant antagonists of our day. Through the prism of the prophetic Word, the climactic occurrences of the last days have been set before us. The problems we can expect have been outlined, giving us a clear pattern with a purpose. This pattern provides a perspective on what has gone before, what God is doing at present, and what He ultimately intends to do to set things right.

In God's Word, and there alone, we find all we need to know for triumphant living in these last days. And the *very* good news is that we can share the triumph of our Lord in our daily lives—regardless of the circumstances.

The little book of 2 Peter is magnificently structured to accomplish this task. This Epistle reveals the dimensions of the problems believers will encounter as we approach the closing phases of history on this planet. Above all, it tells us what we must do so we can overcome the recurrent obstacles placed before us. Interestingly, we must begin, not at the beginning, but at the conclusion of what Peter says through the Holy Spirit:

> *But [you] grow in grace, and in the knowledge of our Lord and Savior, Jesus Christ. To him be glory both now and forever* (3:18).

In one way or another, the apostle repeatedly pressed home the point that his words are intensely personal and must be personally applied. The late and much-revered evangelist Vance Havner once told the story of a woman who entered the office of a psychiatrist. The lady had a strip of bacon over each ear and a fried egg on top of her head.

"Madam, how can I be of assistance to you?" asked the psychiatrist.

The oddly attired woman replied, "I'm here to talk to you about my brother."

Obviously, a bit of conversation about herself may have been in order. This apocryphal tale underscores a point that Peter's Epistle urges on every believer: This message applies to *you*. Don't *you* miss it."

A Revival of Commitment to the Word of God

Through Peter, God commands each of us to keep growing in both the "grace, and in the knowledge of our Lord and Savior, Jesus Christ." The knowledge spoken of here is the full and complete knowledge of God that we can obtain only from the Scriptures. Such knowledge is indispensable to spiritual growth. Unfortunately, one of the great failures among evangelical Christians today is indifference toward studying the Bible in a consistent, systematic way. It seems that entertainment, emotional-ism, and a variety of companion distractions have spawned a biblical illiteracy that is strangling this genera-tion of believers. If we are to function effectively in these last days, we must return to the Book.

The apostle Peter was writing to people beset by an assortment of very serious trials in the first century. They were being attacked, bloodied, and harassed on multiple fronts. But Peter had a word for them—one that could carry them through as individuals and as a church. His Epistle provided the assurance that God had not forgotten them. Indeed, God had a message for people caught in the storm of hostility whipped up by relentless, religious fanaticism and the marauding degeneracy of pagan Rome.

Their hope was not simply to make it through the per-petually bad circumstances. Rather, theirs was a hope that transcended the veil of this life. They were given a glorious look into eternity. They had a promise. The Lord was coming; and in the end, everything would be all right. In spite of all they were going through, believers were being held safely in the hand of a sovereign God who directed them by His guiding Spirit. His sufficiency secured all of their tomorrows.

Here, too, is our hope: That same sufficiency is available to us every hour of every single day. That is why the words of 2 Peter are inestimably valuable—indispensable, actual-ly—if we are to cope with what surely lies ahead and make a "certain sound" when we share our faith with others.

For example, during the days of the former Soviet Union, a poor Christian peasant met a Communist intellectual in a Moscow train station. Learning that the peasant was a believer in Christ, the intellectual began to ridicule him as ignorant for believing in the existence of God. The intellectual was convinced that God was but a cruel invention of unscrupulous men who wished to control the unenlightened masses. For him, the State represented all that might be regarded as a god. Beyond that, there was nothing.

The peasant listened patiently, complimented the man for his apparent wealth of knowledge, and then commented, "But I have one very big advantage over you."

"What could possibly give you an advantage over me?" the Communist asked.

"My advantage is this: I know what my future is. You have no idea what yours will be."

Those few words, seasoned with a further explanation of why the peasant could make such a statement, ultimately brought the Communist face to face with his need of the Savior.

That is what we call hitting the nail on the head. We know what the future holds, and that precious information tempers everything we experience in life. It also should affect everything we say to others who have not the same hope.

A PREVIEW OF THINGS TO COME

Let's take a quick walk through 2 Peter and see what God has in store for us.

A LOOK AT OURSELVES

In the first chapter, the Lord beckons us to stop and take a good look at ourselves. After all, that usually is an excellent place to begin. Although introspection can be rather unpleasant, it is necessary nonetheless. Only when we have the courage and wisdom to look inside ourselves can we begin the process of growth in grace and knowledge of the

Lord. We shall never be perfect in this life. We are, however, in the process of moving on to full maturity as believers—coming of age as full-grown Christians. That is the concept Peter is dealing with in this first chapter.

Furthermore, his admonitions project a totally positive perspective. His deep love for those he wishes to enlighten is everywhere obvious. And although negative conduct sometimes must be addressed and corrected, Peter does not do so here. Chapter 1 urges us to see ourselves as God sees us and to discover, then develop the gifts He has bestowed. The process almost parallels that of Jesus and the disciples when He spoke to the Samaritan woman at the well. The disciples saw only the worst in someone else, as did the woman who had worn bacon on her ears and an egg on her head. But our Lord looked at the Samaritan woman through different eyes—eyes filled with compassion.

A Look at Our Adversaries

In chapter 2, Peter admonishes us to take a good, long look at our adversaries—those who profess to be emissaries of the true and living God but, in reality, are children of the wicked one.

We live in a day when satanic manifestations and agents of evil run loose as never before. Psychics are actually regarded as credible and respectable. Satanism has made tremendous inroads among our young people. And while the government works overtime to shield students in our public institutions from hearing about God and His world, it sees no problem in exposing them to heavy doses of the occult and the world of the Devil.

A few years ago it would have seemed strange indeed to hear of such things going on in America and the Western world. Although occultism and spiritism have always been around, they generally seemed to attract only the credulous and gullible who hovered on the fringes of the basic social fabric.

I remember when a group of people in our small town in Michigan clandestinely visited the haunts of spiritualists in Detroit in order to participate in seances and meet real live mediums. They returned to regale young children with tales of tearing wallpaper, ominous thumps on the ceiling, trumpets flying through the air, and filmy shadows of the departed floating in a ghostly procession through the room. It was all good fun until you were alone in your bed at night, and the winter winds formed moving, finger-like images of leafless trees through your moonlit, upstairs window. By morning you knew again there was nothing to it. A few people (who should have known better) had paid for the privilege of being hoodwinked by a minor-league charlatan. But that was then, and this is now. How things have changed.

Years after my brush with old bed sheets and pseudosorcerers, I took my first trip to Haiti in the West Indies. There I had my first encounter with voodoo. Frankly, I was rather taken aback by the attitude of my missionary friends who tended to give a wide birth to places where voodoo was practiced. I remembered that in churches in the United States, we had heard missionaries from Africa speak of the devil bush and the repulsive things done there. At the time, I wondered how they could imagine that any real demonic power existed in such rituals practiced in the 20th century. The reason for my skepticism was simple: I had never seen overt manifestations of satanic power at home in the United States. Since visiting a number of mission fields around the world, however, I have changed my views.

Satanic power seems to manifest itself most boldly in cultures where the power of the Spirit of God has diminished. Where there are fewer genuine believers, there is more satanic activity. What formerly was not true in much of the Western world, including the United States, is today a fact of life. As the manifestation of the power of God diminishes in believers (perhaps because there are fewer true believers), occult powers and practices become more evident.

Unveiling before our eyes is the spirit of the age, which God told us to expect as the last days come on us. The apostle John characterized it as the spirit of Antichrist. He wrote,

> Little children, it is the last time [hour]; and as ye have heard that antichrist shall come, even now are there many antichrists, by which we know that it is the last time [hour] (1 Jn. 2:18).

It is the beginning of the end-times.

Jesus also warned that during the Tribulation period, after the church has been raptured, many false Christs will appear to deceive and lead astray the vast majority of people on Earth at the time:

> Then if any man shall say unto you, Lo, here is Christ, or there; believe it not. For there shall arise false Christs, and false prophets, and shall show great signs and wonders, insomuch that, if it were possible, they shall deceive the very elect. Behold, I have told you before. Wherefore, if they shall say unto you, Behold, he is in the desert; go not forth: behold, he is in the secret chambers; believe it not (Mt. 24:23–26).

According to these Scriptures, we are, at the very least, living in a time when many antichrists are arriving on the scene. Although we are not now in the Tribulation period, we nevertheless can expect an onslaught of false teachers. Waving the banner of Christianity, these deceivers will wear a variety of guises and promote heresies and apostasy while claiming to speak in the name of God. Of course, they will not be of God. In the process, they will deceive and delude countless thousands, perhaps millions, of people.

Here in 2 Peter 2, the Lord gives us what perhaps is the clearest exposition in the entire Bible of a false teacher. He also exposes us to the devastation caused by these pseudoemissaries of the Lord who live at the expense of the church while ravaging the body of Christ. Their mission, crafted by Satan, is to bring a lost world to the place where Adam's children will eagerly embrace the Big Lie—that man can live independently of God.

We can be grateful we have been forewarned because only then shall we be able to stand against the wiles of the enemy.

A LOOK AT OUR FUTURE

Chapter 3 turns our attention to the future. In the last dismal days before the Rapture of the church, our Lord does not leave us comfortless or ill equipped. We have a hope. Better said, we have the "Blessed Hope." For before the fires of the Tribulation rise, we shall find ourselves in the presence of our Savior. This is His promise by way of the apostle Paul:

> *Teaching us that, denying ungodliness and worldly lusts, we should live soberly, righteously, and godly, in this present age, Looking for that blessed hope, and the glorious appearing of the great God and our Savior, Jesus Christ, Who gave himself for us that he might redeem us from all iniquity, and*

purify unto himself a people of his own, zealous of good works (Ti. 2:12-14).

This snatching-away of believers before the Time of Jacob's Trouble (Tribulation) is an important fact of life for those of us who look for the imminent, any-moment appearance of our dear Savior. Yet we do not view as enemies those friends who believe the church will suffer through various stages of the Tribulation. However, we differ emphatically with their pessimistic appraisals of future events. Such positions endorse a kind of Protestant purgatory, totally missing the mark when it comes to God's plan for His people. As believers, we have a star on our horizon. We view what is now unfolding in a way like Abraham of old, who "looked for a city which hath foundations, whose builder and maker is God" (Heb. 11:10).

In our case, we look for the Maker of the City, who will transport us to that luxuriously prepared place He has fashioned for His own. For He tells us that, as His pilgrim people, we are to do His bidding and move ahead while we keep looking up. Therefore, in the most wonderful sense of the word, the best is yet to come.

A PORTRAIT OF GOD'S MAN

To begin with, let us briefly consider the man God chose to bring this marvelous little book to us. Simon Peter exemplifies the divine genius for creating unity out of diversity—the kind of unity one would not expect from the tapestry of humanity that characterizes the early followers of Christ.

A great and encouraging lesson resides here for all of us. For once we truly learn that the penmen of Scripture were men with passions, frailties, and failures like our own, we can begin to accept what we can become in His hand and for His glory. Peter is a prototype:

> *Simon Peter, a servant and an apostle of Jesus Christ, to them that have obtained like precious faith with us through the righteousness of God and our Savior, Jesus Christ* (1:1).

Considering where Peter was when God found him, such a statement is rather astonishing. Peter, after all, was a brawling fisherman with a propensity to put his foot in his mouth and say the wrong thing at the wrong time. It was Peter who slept in the Garden of Gethsemane when he should have been awake. He was often distracted when he should have been paying attention. His answer to an enemy of the Lord was to slash off the man's ear with a sword. God undoubtedly had a lot of work to do on Peter before he could rightly be called "a servant and an apostle of Jesus Christ."

It has always intrigued me that so many of us are attracted to the apostle Peter. We seem to gravitate to his personality—imperfections and all. The reason may well be that so many of us are so much like him, although we may not like to think so. Actually, it is a great encouragement to examine Peter's transformation and see what God may want to teach us. We, too, can be changed to become the people He wants us to be. After all, one of the great joys of the Christian life is witnessing what God, in His omnipotence, is able to do with the most unlikely of souls—often to our surprise. He is not just the God of the lovely; He is the God of the unlovely as well. And it might be good to pause and see which category we fall into.

The record of Peter's transformation is one of the great human stories in Scripture. Matthew 19 is a focal point. A man known as the rich young ruler asked Jesus a question:

> *And, behold, one came and said unto him, Good Master, what good thing shall I do, that I may have eternal life? And he said unto him, Why callest thou me good? There is none good but one, that is, God; but if thou wilt enter into life, keep the commandments* (vv. 16–17).

When Jesus recited a number of them, the rich young man replied,

> *All these things have I kept from my youth up. What lack I yet? Jesus said unto him, If thou wilt be perfect, go and sell what thou hast, and give to the poor, and thou shalt have treasure in heaven; and come and follow me. But when the young man heard that saying, he went away sorrowful; for he had great possessions* (vv. 20–22).

At issue with the young man was adequate compensation. How much or, perhaps, how little of his wealth could he afford to give up and still qualify for eternal life? When Jesus told him to give up *everything*, it was more than the young man could handle. In actuality, he was trying to enter heaven from the wrong road—the route of material possessions. His mistake was the same as that of millions of others throughout the centuries. Salvation is far beyond anything money can buy. It is secured by faith, not by lucre.

After the disappointed youth departed, Peter raised a question:

> *Then answered Peter and said unto him, Behold, we have forsaken all, and followed thee. What shall we have, therefore?* (v. 27)

The fisherman's query was perfectly legitimate. He was a man driven by a well-honed work ethic: A man worked; a man received payment for his toil. Peter simply wanted to know what was in it for him—nothing wrong with that. At this stage in his life, he thought as a natural man did, not like a regenerated one. What do I get for what I give? This was Peter before Pentecost.

His story broadens based on two events. The first was his nocturnal walk across the whitecaps one stormy night on the Sea of Galilee. Following the feeding of the 5,000, the disciples were sent away toward Capernaum while Jesus stayed behind to pray.

Amid a fierce storm, the Lord arrived, walking to them on the water.

> *And when the disciples saw him walking on the sea, they were troubled, saying, It is a ghost; and they cried out for fear. But straightway Jesus spoke unto them, saying, Be of good cheer; it is I; be not afraid. And Peter answered him and said, Lord, if it be thou, bid me come unto thee on the water. And he said, Come. And when Peter was come down out of the boat, he walked on the water, to go to Jesus. But when he saw the wind boisterous, he was afraid; and beginning to sink, he cried, saying, Lord, save me. And immediately Jesus stretched forth his hand, and caught him, and said unto him, O thou of little faith, why didst thou doubt?* (Mt. 14:26–31).

Peter had leaped out of that fishing craft as a cocksure son of the sea. But the fury of the storm reduced him to a drowning fisherman crying to his Lord for help. His words, "Lord, save me" (Mt. 14:30), represent a profound change that was taking place in his life, the dramatic dimensions of which would soon shake the known world.

Following the feeding of the 5,000, the miraculous walk on the water, and Peter's encounter with the sea, Jesus taught in the synagogue at Capernaum. The religious intelligentsia was, to say the least, unimpressed. After Jesus had made the point that a right relationship to Him was more important than baskets full of bread and fish, the multitudes melted away like snow before the sun and winds of spring. Dejected, the disciples saw their hopes fading with the ebbing crowd. Then He asked them a question—one by one, I think.

> From that time many of his disciples went back, and walked no more with him. Then said Jesus unto the twelve, Will ye also go away? Then Simon Peter answered him, Lord, to whom shall we go? Thou hast the words of eternal life. And we believe and are sure that thou art that Christ, the Son of the living God (Jn. 6:66-69).

Peter's answer emanated from the depths of his encounter among the waves of the Galilee. On that evening, Peter, in a sense, had sunk under the water as a drowning fisherman and had emerged an apostle of God. True, he had not yet experienced Pentecost, and he still had numerous imperfections. But the Galilean was a changed man. That dark night he had listened and had heard all he needed to hear. This Messiah, this Jesus of Nazareth, was now etched on his heart and mind in a unique and wonderful way.

Just how thorough was Peter's transformation? We find the answer as we follow him and the apostle John as they ascend the steps to the Beautiful Gate of the Temple in Jerusalem.

> *Now Peter and John went up together into the temple at the hour of prayer, being the ninth hour. And a certain man, lame from his birth, was carried, whom they laid daily at the gate of the temple which is called Beautiful, to ask alms of them that entered into the temple; Who, seeing Peter and John about to go into the temple, asked an alms. And Peter, fastening his eyes upon him, with John, said, Look on us. And he gave heed unto them, expecting to receive something from them. Then Peter said, Silver and gold have I none, but, such as I have, give I thee. In the name of Jesus Christ of Nazareth, rise up and walk"* (Acts 3:1-6).

The man who had said, "What shall I have?" was now saying to a lame beggar, "Such as I have, I give"! The getter became the giver.

These three great events turned the rugged fisherman into the emissary of God, "a servant and apostle of Jesus Christ."

What God did for Peter, He can do for each of us.

CONCLUSION

We Christians often accomplish less than we should in the service of Christ because we are self-intimidated. We sometimes view ourselves as ill equipped, for a variety of reasons. It may be due to a lack of education or an inability to communicate effectively. Early in his life, Peter had more liabilities than assets. His amazing transformation under the power of the Holy Spirit should encourage each of us to strive to be all that He designs for our lives. The Lord is the all-sufficient enabler; our responsibility is merely to be available to Him.

REMEMBERING FIRST THINGS   2

*Grace and peace be multiplied unto
you through the knowledge of God,
and of Jesus, our Lord* (1:2).

While en route to ministering at a conference in the Northwest one year, I passed a church with a sign out front that caught my eye. It advertised "19–minute sermons." I thought about that sign for the rest of my drive. Were 19 minutes all the pastor could deliver, or were they all the congregation could take? Whatever the answer, the advertisement seemed a rather depressing sign of the times.

Why is it that so many of us become impatient when we hear something repeated from the pulpit more than once? You can almost hear people begin to whisper, "Isn't he spending enough time in study? Maybe he is showing early signs of senility." For some reason, most people in the pews today demand that their Sunday morning fare be delivered in a quick, painless, and entertaining way. They would not be at all happy with the methodology of the apostle Peter.

Fortunately, Peter was cut from a different cloth. He saw the value of reiteration and was determined to persevere in

*repeat
again
&
again*

stressing the importance of first things so they could take hold in peoples' lives.

To understand Peter's purpose in writing this Epistle, we must remember Peter's background and that his life and ministry had turned emphatically from focusing on what he could get to "such as I have, I give."

Throughout the Epistle, he stirs up the minds of the saints through constant reminders, directing his readers in all generations to maintain or rekindle their first-love relationships with the Lord:

> *Wherefore, I will not be negligent to put you always in remembrance of these things, though ye know them, and are established in the present truth. Yea, I think it fitting, as long as I am in this tabernacle, to stir you up by putting you in remembrance* (1:12–13).

His instruction rests on three factors:

1. Remember the words of the prophets.
2. Remember the commandments of the Lord.
3. Remember His words as transmitted by the apostles.

Thus Peter tells us to search the Scriptures tenaciously—the Old Testament, the Gospels, and the Epistles. In them, we shall find the fulfilling relationship that the Lord promises His followers.

Taking the liberty to remind us of what we should already know, Peter reinforces principles basic to our growth, development, and worship relationship to the Savior. In addition, he keeps us on track with respect to the fundamental aspects of our faith and the mission to evangelize, particularly as they relate to life in these last days. Realizing how short the attention span of many end-times

Christians will become, Peter boldly repeats himself. Is so much repetition necessary? Apparently so. But is it welcome? Not always.

In the late 1800s, a man named John Jasper was converted to Christ while a slave on the plantation of a prominent Richmond, Virginia, family. After the Civil War, he gained his freedom and became a great preacher. He pastored the Sixth Mount Zion Baptist Church in the city. John Jasper possessed a magnificent gift for preaching the Word with eloquence and power. He also had an interesting way of repeating himself. In fact, Rev. Jasper repeated himself so often he even used the same outlines, illustrations, and stories. One day a dissatisfied parishioner spoke with him on the subject.

"Pastor Jasper," he said, "we notice you have a habit of preaching your sermons over and over again. You use the same passages of Scripture—same everything. The people know your messages about as well as you do. We want to know why it is you do this?"

Pastor Jasper leaned back to think it over for a moment.

"Well," he answered, "that's easy. You see, there are some sermons I just like to hear me preach again. And as long as I'm blessed and my people receive a blessing, I guess I'll just go on and preach them over again."

It was a good answer. But beyond the ability to give good answers, John Jasper was an exceptionally perceptive man. He knew his people needed to hear central propositions of the Word repeatedly until those principles began to shape their lives and their walks with the Lord.

A few years ago, we heard a considerable amount of conversation about "getting back to basics." The phrase rang of a worthy enterprise. However, if we truly tried to return to basics, I fear many Christians probably would not know where to begin. Here is where the apostle Peter can help. He not only knew the basics, he knew exactly where to find them.

LIKE PRECIOUS FAITH

> *Simon Peter, a servant and an apostle of Jesus Christ, to them that have obtained like precious faith with us through the righteousness of God and our Savior, Jesus Christ: Grace and peace be multiplied unto you through the knowledge of God, and of Jesus, our Lord, According as his divine power hath given unto us all things that pertain unto life and godliness, through the knowledge of him that hath called us to glory and virtue (1:1–3).*

These foundational verses expose the essence of our faith—its quality, scope, substance, and source. In so few words, Peter provides all we need to live triumphantly in these last days. Furthermore, he treats us to an awe-inspiring bit of information: The faith we possess because of our relationships with Jesus Christ is equal in measure and quality to that of the apostles themselves. Peter writes "to them that have obtained **like precious faith** [emphasis added]" (1:1).

"Like precious faith" or, if you will, "faith of the same kind," actually means that God gives all believers the same faith and the same Christian privileges. Just think of it: The identical faith, in measure and quality, that fueled the lives of such men as Paul, Peter, James, and John, as well as other great Christians throughout history, belongs to you and me. What a standard! Our faith is a marvelous prism through which must pass everything else Peter says in this chapter. Thus God has good news for us: Christianity has no second-class citizens in the faith!

This fact should come as a great word of encouragement in a day when so many believers have become star-struck by "superluminaries" in the Christian church. In many respects, we help create these "heroes"; then we shrink meekly before them into lives dwarfed and intimidated by their much-heralded greatness. Alongside them, we often feel inadequate. Indeed, some of us have become so self-deprecating that we settle for being far less than God intends us to be.

But here again is good news. Your faith is of equal kind and quality as theirs. Consequently, you enjoy every privilege available through the finished work of Christ. And though others may stand more prominently on the stage than you, your mission is every bit as valuable and rewarding in God's eyes as theirs is.

I learned this principle through a man I knew in my early days as pastor of a small rural church in Virginia. My friend had grown up in an extremely difficult situation. Many members of his family were alcoholics who took a dim view of formal education. Consequently, he never went past the first grade. However, within that dysfunctional family was a good and godly woman, his mother. Humanly speaking, the odds were against this lonely woman living long enough to see her child come to know and love God as she did.

When her son was four or five, she would start each day by taking him down the path to the spring where she fetched a pail of water every morning. When they reached an aging pear tree, she would put down her pail; get down on her knees; and, with the boy at her side, pray for his salvation.

As the boy grew, his mother seemed to lose the battle for his soul. By the time he reached his early teens, he had become a confirmed alcoholic. By then he had no mother to try and guide him down the right path. He had only a group of sawmill workers who had no interest whatever in the "good life" a Christian was expected to live.

But his mother's influence did not die with her. He later told me that when he was at his lowest point, often falling on his rumpled bed in a drunken stupor, she was there.

"In my mind's eye," he said, "I could see her, with me at her side, down on her knees praying for me. I could never get that out of my mind." Soon he felt a deepening desire to find what it was his mother had had—he wanted to be saved.

One morning, in a neatly painted, white, clapboard-sided church, he startled the congregation when he walked in the door and took a seat. When the pastor gave the invitation, the young alcoholic walked down the aisle to receive Christ as his personal Savior.

Following his conversion, he began to grow mightily in the Lord. Unable to read, he asked his pastor to mark important passages in his Bible in red. He particularly wanted verses related to the theme of salvation. Then he had others read aloud those marked Scriptures, and he would share his faith. Over the years, this illiterate and socially deprived man became one of the most respected persons in the community. People seldom spoke about what it meant to be a real Christian without his name entering the conversation.

When touched by God's grace, this most unlikely candidate for sainthood manifested a faith of the same quality as that of any apostle. The same potential exists for all of us who have believed.

Peter, after all, was transformed from an unworthy, faltering, frail human being into an apostle of God. The work of Jesus Christ changed him so radically that he was hardly the same man during the later stages of his life. And through Peter, God tells us things about ourselves that every one of us should consciously appropriate every day of our lives. These truths are the solid stuff of God's grace, which He freely bestows on the life of every sinner who believes.

HIS RIGHTEOUSNESS ALONE

The foundation of Peter's Spirit-inspired Epistle is laid before us here: This "like precious faith" is obtained exclusively "through the righteousness of God and our Savior, Jesus Christ" (1:1).

Peter is saying, "First things first." If we miss this point, the rest of the Epistle may as well be an empty page. The righteousness that opens every successive door is the righteousness of Jesus Christ Himself—imputed to the believer. As we trust Him and His finished work for us on Calvary, we are made wholly righteous in the eyes of God. Some oft-quoted words from Paul's Epistle to the Ephesians express this concept beautifully:

> For by grace are ye saved through faith; and that not of yourselves, it is the gift of God—Not of works, lest any man should boast. For we are his workmanship, created in Christ Jesus unto good works, which God hath before ordained that we should walk in them (Eph. 2:8–10).

By grace, we have received His righteousness as our own and have been given attributes displaying the fact that we are indeed the "workmanship" of God,"created in Christ

Jesus." In plain terms, even after becoming believers, we do what we do because we are what we are.

Life and Godliness

Because He has saved us, we now have a new scope of possibilities open to us, "according as his divine power hath given unto us all things that pertain unto life and godliness" (1:3). The phrase *all things* is an astonishing revelation. Every aspect of life on this planet and godliness before the Lord and men are available to us. The question is, How much of this provision are we willing to appropriate?

In a way, we could compare this endowment to the vast capacity for knowledge and function we possess in our brains in relation to how very little we actually put to use. We face a great challenge here. God explicitly tells us that "all things that pertain unto life and godliness" are ours for the taking. How much, however, have we chosen to reach out and take? We may back away from this challenge by claiming we do not know all we need to know in order to be all that we should be. However, the Lord has an answer for that problem too.

Knowledge, Glory, Virtue

If we need knowledge (and we do), God has done something wonderful for us. He has made available to us the "knowledge of him." Peter refers here to the *full and complete knowledge of God*, transmitted to us in a very specific way: through the agency of His Word—and His Word alone.

Today many competing and often conflicting "authorities" claim to receive direct revelation from God. In some respects, they tout a sort of "hot line to heaven," which many people find attractive. These "authorities" claim that

God makes truth known as He speaks directly, sometimes audibly, to people who then channel His words to the rest of us. This theory, however, presents a big problem and an uncertain prospect: How do we determine who actually is giving us a true word from the Lord? And when one person's messages conflict with another's, as they often do, whom are we to believe?

I once heard a man say that God often spoke to him audibly—a revelation that startled many in the audience.

"But you know," he said, "most often when the Lord speaks to me, His voice sounds just like my wife!"

After the meeting, many people seemed to agree that his wife, not the Lord, was issuing the orders.

This story may seem somewhat crude, but it reveals an important point. God, in His infinite wisdom, foresaw what would take place in the last days. As in the time of the great Tower of Babel, many tongues will compete for spiritual supremacy. And, as Jesus warned, many who are emissaries of another master will come, claiming to be speaking in the name of God. In anticipation of this fact and for other reasons known only to Himself, the Lord today confines His direct revelation to the Scriptures. Although nature speaks of the reality of God and provides a magnificent witness to His power, we can learn His identity and subsequent plan for His creation only through the Word.

Peter places great emphasis on the supremacy of the Word of God. In verse 16 of chapter 1, he introduces his own experience on the Mount of Transfiguration with Jesus, James, and John. "For we have not followed cunningly devised fables," he assures us, "but were eyewitnesses of his majesty." Verse 17 reveals that the wide-eyed disciples were privy to an unprecedented event. Jesus was glorified before them; and in that remarkable circumstance, they heard the audible voice of the Father saying, "This is my beloved Son, in whom I am well pleased" (Mt. 17:5). In His glorification, they received a prophetic preview of the King and His coming Kingdom. Therefore, Peter shares with them "the power and coming of our Lord Jesus Christ" (v. 16). He says much more about the coming of the Lord in chapter 3. Now, however, Peter lays the ground-work for an immense proposition—one expressly meant for those of us who are witnessing the prelude to the Lord's promised return. He informs us this way:

> *We have also a more sure word of prophecy, unto which ye do well that ye take heed, as unto a light that shineth in a dark place, . . .Knowing this first, that no prophecy of the scripture is of any private interpretation. For the prophecy came not at any time by the will of man, but holy men of God spoke as they were moved by the Holy Spirit* (1:19–21).

No prophecy of Scripture accommodates "any private interpretation." That is, no single prophecy stands on its own or, for that matter, originates with any source other than God Himself. Therefore, true prophecy is never isolated from the rest of the body of prophetic Scripture found in the Word. Such is the pure genius of divine revelation. Although a host of "holy men of God" from a variety of time-oriented, polit-ical, and cultural conditions wrote as they were directed by the Holy Spirit, not one iota of contradiction exists in all of the body of Scripture penned by their hands.

To you and me, who were not on the Mount of Transfiguration with Peter, James, and John, God has given an abiding and sustaining reality. It is "a word of prophecy" made more sure, meaning the Scriptures we hold in our hands today. These Scriptures are as inspirational, enlightening, and encouraging as being an eyewitness to His glory on the mount. Their "sure" words provide a light and compass for us as we move ever further into the darkness that is gathering about us.

The apostle Paul's words to Timothy echo Peter's:

> All scripture is given by inspiration of God, and is profitable for doctrine, for reproof, for correction, for instruction in righteousness, That the man of God may be perfect, thoroughly furnished unto all good works (2 Tim. 3:16–17).

With the full knowledge of God at our disposal, we have been called "to glory and virtue" (v. 3), that is, to reflect *His* glory and virtue. In our Lord's great high priestly intercessory prayer for believers, He said, "And the glory which thou gavest me I have given them" (Jn. 17:22). Here is the substance of what we are told in the first chapter of 2 Peter. All virtue and glory resplendent in the lives of believers are, in actuality, Christ's own, shining through us.

To explain this truth, someone once compared Christians to the moon and God to the sun. The moon itself has no radiance. It only reflects the glory of the sun. We, too, are reflectors, radiating the virtue and glory of the Son of God.

ALL THINGS THAT PERTAIN TO LIFE AND GODLINESS

> *By which are given unto us exceedingly great and precious promises, that by these ye might be partakers of the divine nature, having escaped the corruption that is in the world through lust (1:4).*

The great and precious promises believers possess are transmitted through His "glory and virtue" (1:3). These promises are a gracious gift from God. Just as salvation is imparted to us through His grace and mercy, so, too, are the divine promises. Even more amazing is that these promises are as certain as if they were already fulfilled. That very fact should have a sanctifying effect on every believer. In the words of one commentator, the promises "assimilate" us to God. We thus become "partakers of the divine nature" (v. 4) if now only in part, but hereafter, fully and forever. In the words of the apostle John, "We shall be like him" (1 Jn. 3:2).

Being partakers of the divine nature, of course, does not imply that we become a part of His essence; rather, we partake of His holiness, which includes His glory and virtue.

Furthermore, we become participants in what one might refer to as "the great escape." The imagery implies escaping from the cell of the condemned. Not only are we set at liberty in Christ, but we also have escaped the ultimate corruption of death and the grave. The "corruption that is in the world" (v. 4) refers not so much to the material universe around us as to the lust perpetually inherent in unsaved individuals.

In just a few magnificent words, the Holy Spirit promises to give us:

- All things that pertain to life and godliness.
- The full and complete "knowledge of God."
- His own glory and virtue.
- Great and precious promises.
- A portion in the divine nature.
- A way of escape from the corruption that is in the world through lust.

How could any of us ask for more?

CONCLUSION

The apostle Peter's opening words clarify several important truths:

(1) Believers should never grow impatient or irritated when reminded of the foundations of the faith. Nor should we disregard the primacy of the preaching of the simple gospel as something too elementary to dignify with our attention.

(2) The absolute authority of the Scriptures must never give way to novel interpretations. Every help available to us—commentaries, experience-related books, study guides, novels, seminar manuals, and the like—are only subsidiary sources. Use these helps in the light of Scripture, never the other way around. Avoid word-of-knowledge claims by people professing to deliver "fresh words from God." Only two sources of revelation exist. Either God is dispensing information or Satan is. Only the "full knowledge of God" as revealed through the Word of God can confirm the validity of the message as being from God.

(3) No second-class citizens inhabit the body of Christ. It is not a one-part organism. This fact is made abundantly clear in the letter of 1 Corinthians:

> That there should be no schism in the body, but that the members should have the same care one for another. And whether one member suffer, all the members suffer with it; or one member be honored, all the members rejoice with it. Now ye are the body of Christ, and members in particular (12:25–27).

The phrase *and members in particular* is crucial. No person or work is insignificant or due less honor than another.

Regardless of what position we hold in the church, we must remember that in the Christian life, superior and inferior are concepts that do not exist.

THEY SHALL NEVER FALL   3

For if these things be in you, and abound,
they make you that ye shall neither be
barren nor unfruitful in the knowledge of
our Lord Jesus Christ (1:8).

For many years I assumed the process of progress in the
faith was comparable to building a spiritual structure. By
placing one element on another, I thought, a Christian
could develop a quality of life that would hold up like a
strong and durable edifice. Although this concept has validity, a much more intimate and expressive process emerges
from the text. The concept here is organic in nature. In 2 Peter
3:18, Peter admonishes believers to "grow in grace, and in
the knowledge of our Lord and Savior, Jesus Christ." Verses
4–7 of chapter 1 are consistent with this admonition.

GROWING CHRISTIANS GOD'S WAY

And beside this, giving all diligence, add to your
faith virtue; and to virtue, knowledge; And to
knowledge, self-control; and to self-control,
patience; and to patience, godliness; And to godli-
ness, brotherly kindness; and to brotherly kind-
ness, love (1:5–7).

The central thought here is that one grace produces another. Each new attribute matures to bring forth another. As a matter of fact, this section can better be read this way: *In your faith,* provide virtue; *in your virtue,* provide knowledge; *in your knowledge,* provide self-control; *in your self-control,* provide patience; *in your patience,* provide godliness; *in your godliness,* provide brotherly kindness; *in your brotherly kindness,* provide love.

Just as a rare and beautiful flower develops from seed to blossom, so, too, spiritual growth progresses from one stage to another until we bloom into mature Christians.

In the apostle Paul's list of the fruit of the Spirit found in Galatians 5, love is placed first. It is the root from which the fullness of the fruit develops: "But the fruit of the Spirit is love, joy, peace, long-suffering, gentleness, goodness, faith, Meekness, self-control" (Gal. 5:22–23).

Peter, however, begins with faith and progresses toward love. In reality, when both sequences are placed side by side, they give us a wonderful picture of God's ability to produce mature, productive, and fully furnished saints. Faith and love each form an end of the spectrum between which we find everything necessary for "life and godliness" (v. 3).

Faith

Faith is that simple yet indispensable provision that invades the life of the sinner who exercises belief in Christ's finished work. Two thousand years ago, a pagan jailer in a place called Philippi raised an anguished question before Paul and Silas: "Sirs," he cried out, "what must I do to be saved?" Paul responded, "Believe on the Lord Jesus Christ, and thou shalt be saved, and thy house" (Acts 16:30–31).

Certainly, during the events of that fateful night in the damp and dark jail, mingled with prayers and songs of praise to God was the proclamation of the gospel. It likely lacked the philosophical eloquence of Paul's speech on Mars' Hill in Athens and was delivered in the straightforward way we find in 1 Corinthians 15. Nevertheless, what the jailer was asked to believe was the gospel Paul faithfully preached:

> That Christ died for our sins according to the scriptures; And that he was buried, and that he rose again the third day according to the scriptures (1 Cor. 15: 3–4).

The message is so simple that no one can miss it. Yet the implications are profound, far beyond anything finite minds can comprehend. For starters, we can ponder 2 Peter 1:4, which says that all believers have been made "partakers of the divine nature." Therefore, we have become escapees, "having escaped the corruption that is in the world through lust."

How fascinating that Peter chooses words that would be well understood by the jailer in Philippi, who was physically free but spiritually in bondage until he was released by faith in Christ. Peter himself had an experience in jail and had miraculously escaped (Acts. 12:1–19). Indeed, Jesus had told a group of men in a synagogue at Nazareth that He had come to set the captives free (Lk. 4:18). All who have come into the faith through Him have experienced the fullness of that freedom.

VIRTUE

Virtue grows out of faith. Remember, this virtue is the very virtue of Christ Himself. Simply defined, it is a proclivity toward being good. Because we have become partakers of the divine nature, virtue should come quite naturally even to newborn Christians. The Bible describes repentance as a change of mind. It also implies a change in direction—to turn again. Paul commended the believers in Thessalonica because they had "turned to God from idols, to serve the living and true God" (1 Th. 1:9). They did not need a seminary course to understand what an idol was. Nor did they need much instruction to see the benefit of turning from them.

Likewise, it is fundamental to the experience of the new birth that we should now become good (virtuous) people. Granted, every believer will encounter formidable hurdles along the track to maturity. Nevertheless, we are to become people who manifest virtue. After all, we are told in Ephesians 2:10 that "we are his workmanship, created in Christ Jesus unto good works, which God hath before ordained that we should walk in them."

In the next growth cycle, we are to appropriate all that being virtuous actually involves.

KNOWLEDGE

Now begins the hard part—embarking on the lifelong search for knowledge. This quest requires moving diligently beyond being generally good to becoming spiritually productive. And it requires hard work. "Giving all diligence" is the standard (v. 5). The call is for each of us to study the Word faithfully—to give ourselves unflinchingly to learning what the Bible says about how we should then live. Unfortunately, too many people are willing to settle for perpetual infancy as Christians because they fail to study the Word of God.

The knowledge referred to here implies an awareness or understanding that is garnered through experience or study, including the total of what has been discovered or learned. It is an all-encompassing inclusion of facts, concepts, understanding, and the entirety of what is known.

Thus knowledge is a wide-ranging grasp of the content and intent of the Word of God and how the Word is translated into the life of the believer. Acquiring knowledge requires a consistent pattern of serious study, which can be an extremely rewarding process that leads to the next stage of growth in grace.

SELF-CONTROL

Infant Christians begin to grow up when they can control their emotions, desires, and actions. Such self-control stems from the progressive growth that only comes in concert with knowledge of the Word. As we begin to grow, we start to manifest the kind of assurance and responsibility that attracts unbelievers to Christ.

When we reach the self-control stage of Christian growth, we approach an important level of maturity by exhibiting the quality of life God desires of us. Admittedly, acquiring self-control can be a hard mountain to climb. Even the disciples, who accompanied our Lord for more than three years, found it difficult. The apostle Paul, in his struggle to subdue self, wrote a classic portion of Scripture that helps clarify the issues we face in the struggle with the "old man":

> For I know that in me (that is, in my flesh) dwelleth no good thing; for to will is present with me, but how to perform that which is good I find not. For the good that I would, I do not; but the

*evil which I would not, that I do. Now if I do that
I would not, it is no more I that do it, but sin that
dwelleth in me* (Rom. 7:18–20).

The adversary Paul faced within himself was the old nature. So extreme was the conflict at times that he used the imagery of the Roman games to describe it. "So fight I," he said, "not as one that beateth the air; But I keep under my body, and bring it into subjection" (1 Cor. 9:26–27).

If you have problems acquiring self-control, you are not alone. In fact, you are in good company. But in the "like precious faith" you share as a believer, you can draw on a common resource—the Lord Jesus Christ. As Paul cried out,

*Oh, wretched man that I am! Who shall deliver me
from the body of this death? I thank God through
Jesus Christ, our Lord* (Rom. 7:24–25).

Appropriating His guidance, leadership, wisdom, etc., is our great resource in striving for self-control. As certainly as we can trust Christ for our salvation, we can rely on Him to deliver us daily from the power of sin.

PATIENCE

Patience grows out of self-control and induces the capacity to endure hardship, difficulty, or inconvenience without complaint. Patience also emphasizes calmness, self-discipline, and the willingness or ability to tolerate delay. It is, therefore, an emblem of growth that manifests the making of true men and women of God.

We have all heard the irreverent, little pseudoprayer, "Lord, give me patience, right now!" Obviously, patience doesn't come that way. It is formed through a tempering process, much like metal is fashioned on the anvil. God uses what we often view as adversity to temper, shape, and skillfully form us into the likeness of Christ.

England's Margaret Thatcher, a conservative politician and former prime minister, was once quoted as saying, "I am extraordinarily patient, provided I get my own way in the end."

Though a trait undoubtedly admired by her peers, her brand of patience does not square with that of the Scriptures. Godly patience is not a tool that impatient people manipulate to their advantage. Nor is it a mask or a façade that temporarily covers some otherwise undesirable characteristic. True patience is the stuff the early Christian martyrs displayed as they stood in arenas while ferocious beasts tore them limb from limb before bloodthirsty pagans who cheered in delight. You cannot fake your way through a situation like that. It is either patience or panic. Certainly, those with genuine patience have found the better way.

Godliness

By definition, godliness has been associated with piety. Its attributes include being saintly, Christlike, and full of grace. Patience and godliness go hand in hand. Godliness springs naturally from patience and the other stages of growth, and it reveals a person at rest in the Lord. Godly people usually are out of sync with their surrounding secular environments but are vitally in touch with God, His Kingdom, and His people.

In 1 Timothy 6:6 we are told, "godliness with contentment is great gain." The passage continues:

> For we brought nothing into this world, and it is certain we can carry nothing out. And having food and raiment let us be therewith content (6:7–8).

Biblical godliness does not encourage laziness in any area of life. The early Christians personified energy and industry and worked tirelessly to take the gospel to the ends of the earth. They also were conscientious in caring for the physical as well as spiritual needs of their brethren. Godly people have a proper view of what is important and what is only relatively so, in contrast to attitudes held by many in the church today. When it comes to amassing worldly goods, godly people know how to say, "It is enough."

One of the godliest individuals I have ever known was a man who lived on the brink of poverty because of a debilitating heart condition. On approaching his house, you never looked in awe at architectural embellishments or well-manicured lawns or gardens. They did not exist. The treasure there was in the man who occupied the ramshackle dwelling.

Never once did I hear him complain about what he did not have. But frequently I heard him speak with great eloquence about the goodness of God and the manifold mercies of his Savior. Here was a truly godly man. And scores of people beat a path to his door just to spend time in his presence and hear him speak on the great themes found in his well-worn Bible. Genuine godliness draws those whose hearts are hungry for the Lord.

Brotherly Kindness

Godly people are disposed toward dealing kindly with their brethren. Without godliness and patience, brotherly kindness is sometimes rather difficult to muster. We sometimes say (and not to our credit) that we love all our brothers and sisters in the Lord; but some are much easier to love at a distance—and the more distance, the better.

Godly believers who have learned patience and brotherly kindness also demonstrate long-suffering. As we shall see in chapter 3, long-suffering is a basic component in God's dealing with each of us in mercy and grace. This fact is certainly true in His bearing with a lost world while He beckons them to turn to Him. For us, brotherly kindness should be an attitude of life. Unfortunately, it is not something most of us possess naturally. Rather, it is a grace that develops out of a life that is firmly rooted in the goodness of God and provision of our Lord Jesus.

Peter, I think, may have had difficulty practicing brotherly kindness when controversy arose. He could be abrasive, even combative, as he was with the apostle Paul during the early development of the church. Nevertheless, he still recognized that he faced a brother. Listen to him speak about Paul:

> *And account that the long-suffering of our Lord is salvation, even as our beloved brother, Paul, also according to the wisdom given unto him hath written unto you* (3:15).

Such graciousness might be the last trait you would expect in a fractious fisherman. But, as I have said, brotherly kindness is a developed grace. And if God could instill it into the life of Peter, He can do so in your life and mine.

LOVE

When the natural growth process produces love within us, we have reached maturity. In the case of plants bearing fruits or vegetables, the blossom heralds the fact that abundant fruit is on the way. Such is the imagery in 2 Peter. Love is depicted as the crowning attribute—the culmination of all the previous stages in a believer's progression toward maturity.

Such love is neither shallow nor emotional. It is a profound, settled, and abiding state of life that reveals all that is to be desired in a thoroughly winsome Christian. In other words, Peter is not talking about a first-stage experience. He is talking about a love that is the sum total of "all things" the Holy Spirit has developed within us "that pertain unto life and godliness" (1:3).

American psychologist Erich Fromm once said this about love: Immature love says, "I love you because I need you." Mature love says, "I need you because I love you." Although Fromm was discussing the human experience exclusively, his assertion that true love is not predicated on selfish need can also be applied to the kind of love God lavishes on His children. His relationship to Israel is an instructive illustration.

"Yea," He declares of Israel, "I have loved thee with an everlasting love; therefore, with loving-kindness have I drawn thee" (Jer. 31:3). We will never fully understand why the Lord loves Israel because we will never be able to search the recesses of the divine mind for the answer. So we must be satisfied to say that, for all we know, He loves the Jewish people because He loves them.

God, of course, does shed a bit of light on His extraordinary love for the sons and daughters of Abraham. But the revelation only seems to deepen the already profound mystery:

> For thou art an holy people unto the LORD thy God; the LORD thy God hath chosen thee to be a special people unto himself, above all people who are upon the face of the earth. The LORD did not set his love upon you, nor choose you, because ye were more in number than any people; for ye were the fewest of all people. But because the LORD loved

> *you, and because he would keep the oath which he had sworn unto your fathers, hath the LORD brought you out with a mighty hand, and redeemed you out of the house of bondage, from the hand of Pharaoh, king of Egypt* (Dt. 7:6–8).

Clearly, the Lord does not need Israel, but He loves her completely and unselfishly anyway—simply because He loves her.

The same principle emerges in the New Testament. Embellishing the most-quoted verse of John 3:16, the apostle John gives us some enlightening and challenging words. This God who so loved us that He gave us His only begotten Son exposes us to our absolute unworthiness and His unqualified love for very unlovely people:

> *In this was manifested the love of God toward us, that God sent his only begotten Son into the world, that we might live through him. Herein is love, not that we loved God, but that he loved us, and sent his Son to be the propitiation for our sins* (1 Jn. 4:9–10).

There you have it. But John has still more to say on the subject. Putting aside all of the lofty and perplexing questions that this concept of God's love for unworthy sinners generates, John quickly returns to where the rubber meets the road: "Beloved, if God so loved us, we ought also to love one another" (1 Jn. 4:11).

Consequently, if we are to love God's children and, I might add, a world of lost sinners who need God, then we must do so in the power of His love as it flows through divinely instilled maturity of life. Second Peter chapter 1 teaches us that, to arrive at this magnificent stage of Christian growth, we must give "all diligence" to the process of preparation.

ABOUNDING IN THE KNOWLEDGE OF THE LORD

For if these things be in you, and abound, they make you that ye shall neither be barren nor unfruitful in the knowledge of our Lord Jesus Christ. But he that lacketh these things is blind and cannot see afar off, and hath forgotten that he was purged from his old sins (1:8–9).

Christians are fond of hearing about the "abundant life." In fact, it is the subject of countless sermons and seminars that too often slip into a litany of the material blessings the Lord is eager to lavish on those of us who will but step up and claim our rights to prosperity. Tragically, many of us in the Western world have become blinded to our fundamental responsibilities because we are so deeply immersed in our affluence. Such a materialistic concept of an abundant life sells only in wealthy societies. It is an outright embarrassment in countries where our brothers and sisters are persecuted or forced to live in squalor and poverty.

The fruit we enjoy as a result of growing in Christ is found not in a multitude of material possessions but in the abundance of the full knowledge of our Lord operating in our lives. This fruit helps us see the things that are "afar off" (1:9). Put another way, it is a sound remedy for poor eyesight and a bad memory.

If you've seen the plethora of television advertisements for herbal medicines, you no doubt have heard that ingesting herbs will cure all kinds of physical and mental ailments. One highly visible ad promises its product will dramatically improve your memory. I'm sure that thousands, perhaps millions, of people have trotted off to the supermarket or drugstore to pick it up. But all the herbal tablets in the world cannot stimulate our spiritual consciousness to remember where we were when God found us and turned us around for eternity. Peter's repeated pleas to remember, if heeded, can deliver us from being "blind" and from forgetting how small we are and how big our God truly is. In addition, remembering how God saved us tends to squash our pride in self and prejudice toward others.

In the last two verses in this section, Peter treats us to a wealth of inspiration for the here and now, as well as for eternity:

> *Wherefore the rather, brethren, give diligence to make your calling and election sure; for if ye do these things, ye shall never fall. For so an entrance shall be ministered unto you abundantly into the everlasting kingdom of our Lord and Savior, Jesus Christ* (1:10–11).

Confirm your calling. That's what the aged apostle is telling his spiritual posterity. Such confirmation comes by manifesting the fruit of the Spirit—godly living that the world can identify as the outgrowth of faith in Christ. The ordinance of baptism provides an apt comparison. Those who have experienced the new birth are commanded to be baptized. Baptism, of course, is not essential to salvation. It is, however, an act of obedience to the Lord and a dramatic demonstration of the spiritual transaction that already has taken place. The newborn child of God is symbolically buried with Christ beneath the water and raised again to walk in newness of life:

> *Therefore, we are buried with him by baptism into death, that as Christ was raised up from the dead*

by the glory of the Father, even so we also should walk in newness of life (Rom. 6:4).

Every person who attends a baptism witnesses, on the physical level, what already has been transacted on a spiritual level through faith in Christ.

When we confirm our spiritual transformation through godly living, we not only demonstrate the reality of our relationship to God but also assure that we will not fall. The word Peter uses for "fall" means to "stumble" or "offend." Godly living will produce a consistent life, free of the roller-coaster ups and downs induced by disobedience, which causes us to stumble.

The fruit of the Spirit, manifested in our lives, provides the basis for rich rewards in eternity and an abundant entrance into heaven.

For so an entrance shall be ministered unto you abundantly into the everlasting kingdom of our Lord and Savior, Jesus Christ (1:11).

The abundance God promises is not in the material realm, where "moth and rust doth corrupt" and where thieves break in to steal from us (Mt. 6:19). His provisions are forever, and His rewards are imperishable and eternal:

For other foundation can no man lay than that which is laid, which is Jesus Christ. Now if any man build upon this foundation gold, silver, precious stones, wood, hay, stubble—Every man's work shall be made manifest; for the day shall declare it, because it shall be revealed by fire; and the fire shall test every man's work of what sort it is. If any man's work abide which he hath built upon it, he shall receive a reward (1 Cor. 3:11–14).

As is true of baptism and confirmation, a believer's reward has nothing to do with salvation. It has everything to do with "treasures in heaven." These rather homely, poetic words put the matter in perspective:

I would not work
My soul to save
For that my Lord
Has done.
But I would work
Like any slave
For love of
His dear Son!

And so we should.

CONCLUSION

The work of the Holy Spirit in our lives can be perfected only through an intimate relationship with the Living Word of God. There is no shortcut. With diligence and a passion to have the mind of Christ, you can enjoy the fruit that only a mature Christian life can yield. Yes, maturity has its price; but the reward is far greater than the cost.

EXODUS   4

Yea, I think it fitting, as long as I am in this tabernacle, to stir you up by putting you in remembrance, Knowing that shortly I must put off this my tabernacle, even as our Lord Jesus Christ hath shown me (1:13–14).

If you want to know what is nearest and dearest to people's hearts, listen to what they say as they step over the threshold to eternity. Following the death in 1981 of Israel's most prominent general, Moshe Dayan, a Hebrew-language newspaper in Jerusalem reported some of his last words: "All my life" the dying general said, "it seems that someone has been following me; and that someone was the Nazarene."

What an astonishing statement, coming from one of Israel's most revered military heroes. It does not imply that Moshe Dayan was a believer in Christ; only God and he have that information. But apparently Jesus of Nazareth significantly occupied Dayan's thoughts during his lifetime, and Dayan felt compelled to include that fact among his last words while still on Earth.

SURVEYING A LIFE OF CHRISTIAN SERVICE

In quite a different way, the apostle Peter also looks back. He surveys his life and ministry and articulates for us a number of points he feels are most important in the light of eternity:

> *Wherefore, I will not be negligent to put you always in remembrance of these things, though ye know them, and are established in the present truth* (1:12).

What preoccupies his mind and fills his thoughts as he prepares to depart this life? Obviously, Peter is not thinking of "religion building," despite the claims of the Roman Catholic Church that he was the first pope and vicar of Christ. In his last days, Peter does not dream of sectarian religious systems, great cathedrals, empty pomp, or splendid ceremonies.

Of deep concern to the apostle are the people he had nurtured in the faith and the events sure to befall them when he dies. He has invested his life in the lives of these early Christians, and he wants assurance that his work will continue. Thus he eagerly stirs their memories to recall first things. He wants believers to lay for themselves a firm foundation in the faith and to build diligently on it, guided by his instructions for the future. He wants his words and influence to remain with them.

In many respects, Peter lovingly nurtured his flock just as the apostle Paul nurtured those whose lives *he* had touched. In an illuminating passage of Scripture found in the Epistle to the Philippians, Paul spoke of his eagerness to leave this earth and pass into the presence of Christ:

> *For me to live is Christ, and to die is gain. But if I*
> *live in the flesh, this is the fruit of my labor, yet*
> *what I shall choose I know not. For I am in a strait*
> *between two, having a desire to depart and to be*
> *with Christ, which is far better* (1:21-23).

Paul was ready to mount the heavenly staircase. In his eyes, to flee into the presence of the Lord was far better than staying in this world of suffering. Two realities filled his mind. The first was his anticipation of the Rapture of the church, which he fully expected to take part in. After describing the resurrection of the bodies of the saints who were "asleep" in death, Paul wrote,

> *Then we who are alive and remain shall be caught*
> *up together with them in the clouds, to meet the*
> *Lord in the air; and so shall we ever be with the*
> *Lord* (1 Th. 4:17).

By saying "we who are alive and remain," Paul obviously included himself. However, he made it clear that he was equally confident of being in the presence of his beloved Savior even if he died before the Lord returned. Since death was preferable, he confessed to being in a "strait between two." His dilemma stemmed from his desire to be with Christ, which he knew was "far better," and his burden to teach believers on Earth, which he knew was necessary.

We often quote Paul's words to those who have seen their loved ones and friends slip from this life. All too often, however, we stop short of reading the entire portion. If we are to know what it means to be truly committed to God's will, we must read the rest of what the former Pharisee had to say because the lesson here is fundamental to the commitment of both Peter and Paul.

"Nevertheless," Paul concluded, "to abide in the flesh is more needful for you" (Phil. 1:24).

As far as he was concerned, Paul was ready and willing to go home to the Lord. But Paul was not operating in the realm of what was best for him in the here and now. He was functioning in the arena of other people's needs. Because they needed him, he was willing to stay. When they no longer needed him, he would eagerly depart this life. The same could be said of Peter, who, in 2 Peter, is more concerned about what he is leaving behind in the lives of his brethren than what he can obtain for his own welfare.

During my years as a pastor, people who were terminally ill sometimes asked me why the Lord allowed them to stay here and suffer. Many of them reasoned that it would be far better for them, and for the loved ones who cared for them, if God would just take them to heaven. Philippians 1:12 gives us a little insight here. It is not for us to question why or for how long God requires our presence on this earth. If we truly believe God is competent and our times are in His hands, we must leave the length of our days to Him.

No matter how far we walk into the valley of the shadow of death or how long we linger there, one thought should occupy our minds: How is God using our situations to touch others? This profound concept should cause us to place a premium on our lives and on our witness that coincides more closely with His plan for us. He is the Alpha and Omega (the beginning and the end) and everything in between; and He orders our lives from our first moments to our last breaths. Thus we can confidently enjoy His perfect peace, regardless of the circumstances around us.

Laying Down Our Tabernacles

> *Yea, I think it fitting, as long as I am in this taber-*
> *nacle, to stir you up by putting you in remem-*
> *brance* (1:13).

Using illuminating imagery, Peter refers to his body as a tabernacle, a tent. His flesh was but a flimsy, temporary dwelling. He sees himself as a pilgrim who is moving toward another destination. Peter knows that one day, his little tent will be folded and put away, and he will ascend into that better country with a city whose builder and maker is God.

Most of us in the affluent West are unfamiliar with tent-dwelling. My home is a short distance from a place in Virginia called Appomattox Court House. There the horrible carnage of the Civil War came to an end. Confederate General Robert E. Lee sat across from Union General Ulysses S. Grant at a small table in a large room in the McLean house. They were negotiating the terms of the surrender of the Army of Northern Virginia. As you read the record of those few climactic days in the history of America, you can sense the pathos both North and South must have felt. The finality of the situation was encapsulated when the orders came for the soldiers to stack their rifles, fold the regimental battle flags, and strike their tents. Striking their tents was the last act of the long and bloody war. It was time to go home. No longer would they be forced to dwell in drafty little tabernacles. Hopefully, each moved on to better things and a life marked by peace and some measure of tranquillity.

That portrait somewhat projects the eternal realities the apostle Peter is explaining. Our physical bodies are, after all, merely tents. One day we will all be ordered to strike them and move on to "a better country." Such has been the hope of believers from time immemorial. It is no less our hope today.

Remembering

Three times in four verses (1:12–15), Peter uses the word *remembrance*. It is an exceedingly strong reminder. The Scriptures tell us,

> *The time will come when they will not endure sound doctrine but, after their own lusts, shall they heap to themselves teachers, having itching ears* (2 Tim. 4:3).

Itching ears compel a person to scratch. The verse describes unstable individuals who flock to a new, Christian curiosity to have their spiritually itching ears temporarily scratched by strange new teaching or doctrine. For this reason, the apostle Paul admonished Timothy, "Preach the word; be diligent in season, out of season; reprove, rebuke, exhort with all long-suffering and doctrine" (2 Tim. 4:2).

No believer should ever tire of being reminded that two major principles of the Christian life are the constant proclamation and subsequent ingestion of God's Word. Yet we often need to be prodded to remember.

Samuel Johnson, British writer and the leading literary figure in the second half of the eighteenth century, said, "People more often need to be reminded than informed." Dr. Johnson probably was correct. Think about it. How much time do we spend reminding our children of what they already know? More information becomes virtually useless until we put to good use what we have already learned. Consequently, Peter charges his hearers to remember, remember, and remember again.

I once had a Greek professor who started almost every class with the same declaration: "The eternal price of knowledge is review, review, review." Frankly, I got good and sick of hearing that phrase. After all these years, however, it still comes back to me. And now I think I have learned something about the meaning of my professor's repetitious admonitions. He likely borrowed them from another, who may himself have borrowed from Peter, a principal propagator of the twin principles of reminder and review.

EXODUS

> *Moreover, I will endeavor that ye may be able, after my decease, to have these things always in remembrance* (1:15).

When referring to his death, Peter uses a word that immediately merits attention. Although translated "decease," the word actually is *exodus*. It is used only one other time in the New Testament; but in the Old Testament, it is a familiar word, which I believer Peter selected with great deliberation.

Exodus literally means "the way out." Peter uses it to speak of his way out of this world and into the immediate presence of Christ. The only other time the word appears in the New Testament is in connection with the transfiguration of our Lord on the mount in the company of Peter, James, and John. It was obviously a word that made a deep impression on the fisherman.

Referring to the experience, Peter states emphatically that he and his companions had seen "the power and coming of our Lord Jesus Christ," and "were eyewitnesses of his majesty" (1:16). Peter had seen with his own eyes the transfigured Messiah. This concept of having eyewitnesses was important in the Jewish culture. At least two eyewitnesses were required to establish credibility in many legal and national situations.

When Paul, for example, spoke of the Savior's resurrection, he carefully documented the number of eyewitnesses to the event:

> And that he was seen of Cephas [Peter], then of the twelve. After that, he was seen of above five hundred brethren at once, of whom the greater part remain unto this present time (1 Cor. 15:5-6).

Having personally witnessed the greatest events in the history of humanity, Peter can therefore say with undeniable certainty that believers in Christ are not following "cunningly devised fables" (1:16).

The account of the transfiguration is found in Luke 9:28–31:

> And it came to pass, about eight days after these sayings, that he took Peter and John and James, and went up into a mountain to pray. And as he prayed, the appearance of his countenance was altered, and his raiment was white and glistening. And, behold, there talked with him two men, who were Moses and Elijah, Who appeared in glory, and spoke of his decease [exodus] which he should accomplish at Jerusalem.

What a momentous event! It was an occasion I would like to see replayed when we get to heaven. These three simple men, Peter, James, and John, must have been awe-struck at the sight of the glorified Christ, flanked by Moses and Elijah, two of the most illustrious men of God in the Hebrew Scriptures. And before them stood their Lord and Master, mantled with the very glory of God. It was as though the *shekinah* glory had descended to rest on Him. The message was clear: God Himself was again tabernacling, or dwelling, among His people—this time in the person of His only begotten Son. Jesus had stepped into time from the throne room in glory, mantled in human flesh. The Father had sent Moses and Elijah to confirm Jesus' right to Messiahship in the company of the two witnesses He had selected.

And what was the topic of the conversation engaged in by Jesus, Moses, and Elijah? They spoke of His "decease"—His exodus— that would be accomplished in Jerusalem. Thus, in his Epistle, Peter repeats what he had heard from Jesus and His companions. Jesus' exodus would be by way of the cross. And I have no doubt that when Peter applies the word to his own exit from the limitations of time and space, he uses it as he had heard it of the Lord. All of the cross work of the Savior—that is, all that was implicit in the work of the Lord in finishing our redemption—is fresh in his mind and vibrant in his heart. And when he uses the word to speak of his own departure, he is identifying with the exodus of his Lord. In fact, the entire scene breathes exodus.

Moses and Elijah

Let's not leave the subject just yet. When we think of Moses, we immediately remember the Exodus from Egypt. Moses was the man God chose to bring His people out of servitude and slavery. It was Moses who led them, under the sheltering blood of the Passover lambs, dry-shod across the Red Sea and onward into the wilderness. For forty years he led the children of Israel on their memorable trek through a barren expanse. Finally they came to the borders of the land promised to father Abraham and his seed. There they stood before their enemies, not as a vast multitude of threadbare immigrants but as a nation of warriors who were ready to possess their possessions. Deuteronomy 6:23 declares God's purpose through all they had endured during their period of preparation: "And he brought us out from there, that he might bring us in, to give us the land which he swore to give unto our fathers."

What a wonderful scenario God sets before us. Moses, the great leader of the Exodus, brought the Israelites out from under the taskmasters' whips to bring them into a better place. They were not delivered to be left languishing in the wilderness. They were brought out to make it possible for them to go in, where they could become all that God designed them to be as a nation.

Peter, no doubt, knew the history of his people and incorporates the essence of the great lessons of the Exodus in his repetitious pleas to us. So he insists that we remember the things we have been taught until they take root in our hearts and lives. And, at the center of it all, we hear the footfalls of the ancient children of Israel reverberating in the skies above the Mount of Transfiguration. Their final exodus was consummated in His exodus from a crude, wooden cross on a skull-shaped hill outside the city walls of Jerusalem. Their Deliverer and ours came to give us a way out of bondage and death. Thus we can say with confidence that we know what exodus is all about, and we have nothing to fear.

The prophet Elijah also stood on that mountain and conversed with our Lord and Moses. And when we think of him, we consider an exodus of another kind:

> And it came to pass, as they [Elijah and Elisha] still went on, and talked, that, behold, there appeared a chariot of fire, and horses of fire, and separated them, and Elijah went up by a whirlwind into heaven (2 Ki. 2:11).

Elijah was almost larger than life during the era of the Old Testament. He did not taste death as we know it. Instead, he rode the famous chariot of fire into the heavens. As the prophet Elisha watched, awaiting his reception of Elijah's mantle, Elijah disappeared. The man who had done battle with the notorious Jezebel and struck down the prophets of Baal would be seen no more in Israel. He had experienced his personal exodus. For Elijah, the way out was the way up.

The event closely parallels the account in the book of Genesis of Enoch, who one day was not found among his brethren. Enoch had suddenly joined the ranks of the missing. But this good and godly man was not lost. The Scriptures tell us what happened: "And Enoch walked with God, and he was not; for God took him" (Gen. 5:24).

Both of these accounts echo with the blessed hope so fondly anticipated by His people in this Age of Grace. As with Enoch and Elijah, our story, too, will one day be told: "They are not here, for they have been taken."

> But we see Jesus, who was made a little lower than the angels for the suffering of death, crowned with glory and honor, that he, by the grace of God, should taste death for every man. For it became

him, for whom are all things, and by whom are all things, in bringing many sons unto glory, to make the captain of their salvation perfect through sufferings. Forasmuch, then, as the children are partakers of flesh and blood, he also himself likewise took part of the same, that through death he might destroy him that had the power of death, that is, the devil, And deliver them who, through fear of death, were all their lifetime subject to bondage (Heb. 2:9–10, 14–15).

Peter knows what his short-term prospects are. "Shortly," he says, "I must put off my tabernacle." But he does not fear, knowing full well he is to enter that excellent glory from which he once heard our Father say, "This is my beloved Son, in whom I am well pleased."

The world-weary, old apostle welcomes his exodus. We, too, may leave this world through death, as did the apostle Peter. Or we may be raptured and find ourselves instantaneously transported into the presence of the Lord—in a moment, in the twinkling of an eye. Either way, may we never forget that our way out has been made possible by His exodus.

CONCLUSION

For those of us who have put our faith and trust in the Lord Jesus Christ, death is not a final enemy. It is but a doorkeeper who, at the time of our departure, opens the gate beyond which lies our eternal home. While we are here, however, we must remember the things that are fundamental to our lives and be obedient to our Savior's commands. As in the case of our Lord and his follower

Peter, we, too, await our exodus. Jesus has given us a glorious "way out." Our way out is the way up. Until that day arrives, we must remain acutely aware of the fact that each of us serves a higher purpose in our relationships with those who need us. And until the Lord releases us from further responsibility to others, we should gladly tarry in this life.

A LOOK AT
OUR ADVERSARIES

But there were false prophets also among the people, even as there shall be false teachers among you, who secretly shall bring in destructive heresies, even denying the Lord that bought them, and bring upon themselves swift destruction (2 Pet. 2:1).

LUST, LUCRE, AND LIES   5

But there were false prophets also among the people, even as there shall be false teachers among you (2:1).

A sharp line of demarcation exists between the first and second chapters of Peter's Epistle. Whereas the first chapter marvelously reveals the positive aspects that grow out of a right relationship with Christ, the second chapter projects the negatives that inevitably result when people willfully reject divine mandates. Individuals who reject biblical truth may proffer themselves as Christian leaders and teachers; but, in fact, they are charlatans and false prophets.

A MORE SURE WORD

We have also a more sure word of prophecy, unto which ye do well that ye take heed, as unto a light that shineth in a dark place, until the day dawn, and the day star arise in your hearts (1:19).

The apostle Peter and his awe-struck companions were eyewitnesses to the glory of their Lord on the mountain; and the experience left a profound impression on them. But as impressive as the sight had been, God was communicating something else as well, the importance of which would go far beyond the limits of that magnificent encounter.

The experience constituted a confirmation—"a more sure word of prophecy." The presence of Moses and Elijah with the Messiah confirmed and reemphasized the relevance of the Old Testament Scriptures and the words of the prophets. The Hebrew Scriptures were not being cast aside for the New Covenant era. Rather, their prophecies would intersect perfectly with the message God would bring through the apostles. Prophecy was not being diminished but being made "more sure."

For those of us who were not privileged to be on the mountain, this "more sure word" confirms that the promises of God endure. And what He promised to Abraham and his descendants only serves to buttress our confidence in the integrity of the entire body of revelation found in our Bibles. Indeed, we "do well to take heed."

THE LIGHT

The phrase *as unto a light that shineth in a dark place* conveys the idea of a torch illuminating a murky room. The light exposes the dirt so someone can then dispose of it. The imagery particularly applies to 2:1, which discusses false teachers. The light of the Word, as nothing else, exposes them and their teachings.

Although we are not currently in the corporeal presence of Christ, we, too, have the light of the Word of God as an infallible guide. The Bible says, "Thy word is a lamp unto my feet, and a light unto my path" (Ps. 119:105).

A verse in Proverbs lends a fascinating dimension to the idea of light shining in dark places: "But the path of the righteous is like the light of dawn, That shines brighter and brighter until the full day" (4:18, NASB).

A fundamental purpose of the Old Testament prophetic Word is to increasingly brighten the pathway of believers as we approach the end of the age and the return of the Messiah. As the world spirals out of control toward the final convulsions of history, the secular intelligentsia will have no true comprehension of what is taking place. The blindness of their hearts has darkened their understanding (Eph. 4:18). Believers, however, should take to heart the words of Christ when we see these events unfold: "And when these things begin to come to pass, then look up, and lift up your heads; for your redemption draweth near" (Lk. 21:28).

THE DAY STAR

Although differing opinions exist regarding the meaning of the phrase *until the day dawn, and the day star arise in your hearts,* it seems clear that, at its base, it refers to the Second Coming of Christ. The Scriptures commonly allude to Christ as the daystar. In Luke 1:78 we read, "Through the tender mercy of our God . . . the dayspring from on high hath visited us." The Bible also says, "But unto you that fear my name shall the Sun of righteousness arise with healing in his wings" (Mal. 4:2).

Jesus Himself makes a defining statement on the subject:

> *I, Jesus, have sent mine angel to testify unto you these things in the churches. I am the root and the offspring of David, and the bright and morning star* (Rev. 22:16).

As believers, we fondly hold in our hearts the sure hope of His coming. Until then, the Word of God illuminates our way and the Holy Spirit empowers and guides us. We have not been left in the dark!

THE SCRIPTURES

> *Knowing this first, that no prophecy of the scripture is of any private interpretation. For the prophecy came not at any time by the will of man, but holy men of God spoke as they were moved by the Holy Spirit (1:20–21).*

The false prophets of the Old Testament era were noted for telling the kings of Israel, as well as the commoners, what they wanted to hear. Throughout Scripture, we see how God used His true prophets to issue scathing denunciations of these charlatans who often led the nation into disaster:

> *Thus saith the LORD of hosts, Hearken not unto the words of the prophets that prophesy unto you. They make you vain; they speak a vision of their own heart, and not out of the mouth of the LORD (Jer. 23:16).*

> *And the word of the LORD came unto me, saying, Son of man, prophesy against the prophets of Israel that prophesy, and say thou unto them that prophesy out of their own hearts, Hear ye the word of the LORD. Thus saith the Lord GOD: Woe unto the foolish prophets, that follow their own spirit, and have seen nothing! (Ezek. 13:1–3).*

The men who penned the Scriptures were different. They did not "speak a vision of their own heart." They did not originate the messages they transmitted because the Word was "not at any time by the will of man." In a somewhat mysterious way, God used men to communicate His message. They were "moved [along] by the Holy Spirit." The term here is a very beautiful maritime expression. It means the prophets and apostles had their sails filled, so to speak, by the breath of the Spirit and were moved along as they recorded His Word. They were not mere mechanisms. In a unique and wonderful way, God cooperated with them while revealing himself through them. The writers retained specific personal characteristics and methods of expression peculiar to each of them. John Calvin expressed the relationship between the writers and their revelations this way:

> He [the Lord] says they were moved, not because they were out of their minds . . . but because they dared nothing by themselves but only in obedience to the guidance of the Spirit, who held sway over their lips as in his own temple.[1]

However, this singular union between the Lord and the writers of the Holy Scriptures ended with the completion of the canon. God has given us His completed Word, and He now expects us to heed it. For people to claim, as do many false teachers, that they are receiving new, divine revelation is no less than blasphemy.

If you rely on the sure Word of God and scrupulously adhere to what God has to say in the Scriptures, you will receive all the constructive instruction and guidance you need. But if you depart from the Word, you will break the line that communicates God's truth. People who profess to be men of truth but lack allegiance to the Bible subject believers and unbelievers alike to the terrible consequences resulting from the repudiation of divine revelation. Perhaps no more distinctive a passage on the subject of false teachers exists than in 2 Peter 2. It provides a chilling chronicle of the damage these faithless, religious practitioners can do.

LIVING WITH THE DEVIL'S COUNTERFEITS

> *But there were false prophets also among the people, even as there shall be false teachers among you, who secretly shall bring in destructive heresies, even denying the Lord that bought them, and bring upon themselves swift destruction* (2:1).

Here Peter exposes the rules by which the emissaries of Satan play their game. Peter forewarns us about the proliferation of false teachers during this period of history. In so doing, he anticipates the perplexity we will experience when encountering so many people who exploit others for their own benefit while perverting the truth of God's Word. The presence of these individuals only means that nothing has changed. What is true today was also true in bygone days. False prophets consistently plagued ancient Israel, attempting to turn the nation from the pathway of God's purpose. Their ilk will also plague believers in the last days. So if you are tempted to think that things have never been so bad, take Peter's advice: Look back, and learn from the past.

THE STORY OF BALAAM

> *[False teachers] have forsaken the right way, and are gone astray, following the way of Balaam, the son of Beor, who loved the wages of unrighteousness (2:15).*

The particulars regarding the way of Balaam are found in Numbers 22—24. Balaam was a man who was well aware of the power of the one true God. We often remember him in connection with his beast of burden. Balaam's donkey spoke to him, and he to the beast. It was, to say the least, a colorful exchange. A talking donkey, however, is not what the story of Balaam is about.

The Israelites had departed Egypt and were making their way to the land Jehovah had promised to them in perpetuity. Balak, king of Moab, and his heathen contemporaries felt threatened by the presence of the Israelites in the region. So Balak turned to someone he evidently felt could curse Israel. The fact that Balak sent emissaries to Balaam "with the rewards of divination in their hand" indicates that the prophet was corrupt (Num. 22:7). This corruption was the way of Balaam. He merchandised his gift for his own benefit. The manner in which Balaam received Balak's lieutenants tells us that he was definitely open to their lucrative proposition:

> *And he [Balaam] said unto them, Lodge here this night, and I will bring you word again, as the Lord shall speak unto me: and the princes of Moab abode with Balaam (Num. 22:8).*

The Lord did speak, and His words should have ended the matter:

> *And God said unto Balaam, Thou shalt not go with them: thou shalt not curse the people; for they are blessed* (Num. 22:12).

Balaam's greed, however, prompted him to persist. And although God, in His permissive will, finally allowed the hireling to go with the Lord's enemies, He nevertheless refused to allow Israel to be cursed. Three times Balaam set up altars, made sacrifices, then prophesied. And each time, the prophecies magnified the God of Israel and foretold what the Lord would do to His enemies through the Chosen People. Above all, God used these prophecies to provide a magnificent view of the coming Messiah:

> *I shall see him, but not now: I shall behold him, but not near: there shall come a Star out of Jacob, and a Scepter shall rise out of Israel, and shall smite the corners of Moab, and destroy all the children of Sheth. And Edom shall be a possession; Seir also shall be a possession for his enemies; and Israel shall do valiantly. Out of Jacob shall he come who shall have dominion* (Num. 24:17–19).

Despite man's worst intentions, God is sovereign and always will prevail. In these most degrading of circumstances, a money-grubbing prophet for hire said much more than he realized—and God again had the last word.

Balaam's failure as a prophet contains three facets.

1. The Way of Balaam (2:15). This aspect speaks of Balaam's eagerness to market his gift for personal profit. By merchandising his prophetic talent, Balaam also intended to garner worldly prestige and power.

2. The Error of Balaam (Jude 11). In reasoning from a

human perspective, Balaam erroneously concluded that because the Israelites manifested evil in their behavior, the Lord would be forced to curse them. Balaam, of course, figured to profit in the process. But he failed to recognize the higher purposes of God's grace through the Messiah and the ultimate realities of the coming Kingdom.

3. The Doctrine of Balaam (Rev. 2:14). Through Balaam's counsel, Balak managed to corrupt the people who could not be cursed (Num. 31:16). Consequently, "Israel joined himself unto Baal-peor; and the anger of the LORD was kindled against Israel" (Num. 25:3). Through intermarriage and idolatry, Israel began to abandon its unique character as a chosen nation and assimilated with its pagan neighbors.

These experiences of ancient Israel contain important lessons for us. Peter points us to the days of Balaam to teach us that nothing ever really changes. Satan is still attempting to thwart the plan of God by using false prophets to sully God's people. Today we not only face more of the same, but an even greater number of false prophets are coming on the scene.

Just as satanic opposition and demonic manifestations were particularly pronounced when Christ was ministering on Earth, so, too, are they today. In fact, in the last days, Satan will unleash his greatest forces of opposition to God, His Christ, and His people.

But there is good news. When Balaam attempted to curse Israel, God overruled and, in the end, triumphed. Ultimately, evil will never win. In our struggle against false teachers and self-professed prophets, we must always remember that God is competent and in control. Satan, in a sense, is on God's leash. He can go only as far as the Lord allows. We can all draw strength from this realization.

The Holy Spirit had a reason for selecting Balaam as an illustration. He is but a single example of what Israel faced continuously. The Old Testament Scriptures abound with stories of the Israelites' encounters with false prophets. Therefore, we do well to study their lives and times so we can understand how they operate and avoid falling into their stealthily laid traps.

DENYING THE LORD

Peter reveals that the end-times false teachers who will prey on Christians will bring with them devastating elements:

> *There shall be false teachers among you, who secretly shall bring in destructive heresies, even denying the Lord that bought them* (2:1).

While oozing sincerity, false teachers are deceitful in their practices because they *secretly* foment heresies. The word *heresy* here denotes a departure from orthodox, biblical interpretation. These heresies are divisive as well as destructive and, at worst, categorically deny the Savior. Such teaching and conduct embody deceit, destruction, and denial.

These intruders and usurpers, of course, are not believers. They are unregenerate men who cloak themselves in a profession of faith as false as their pernicious teachings. Peter bluntly and vividly describes this type of impostor:

> *But it is happened unto them according to the true proverb, The dog is turned to his own vomit again; and the sow that was washed, to her wallowing in the mire* (v. 22).

Peter borrows from an equally vivid and illuminating statement in the book of Proverbs:

> As a dog returneth to his vomit, so a fool returneth to his folly. Seest thou a man wise in his own conceit? There is more hope of a fool than of him (26:11–12).

False teachers who are wise in their own conceits see themselves as the center and circumference of life. Self-loving, self-serving, self-aggrandizing, they become creators of their own calamity and, in the end, "bring upon themselves swift destruction" (2:1).

Peter returns to the barnyard to embellish his depiction. The picture he draws of "the sow that was washed," returning "to her wallowing in the mire" is particularly applicable (2:22). Everything about false teachers is superficial and external. Their "credibility" rests solely on the basis of what they appear to be, not what they really are. In matters pertaining to God and godliness, however, no one, not even the cleverest, most skilled practitioner of deceit, can bluff his way past a God who sees beyond the external. The prophet Samuel learned this truth when he came to Jesse looking for the man God had chosen to be king:

> But the LORD said unto Samuel, Look not on his countenance, or on the height of his stature, because I have refused him [David's brother Eliab]; for the LORD seeth not as man seeth; for man looketh on the outward appearance, but the LORD looketh on the heart (1 Sam. 16:7).

Jesus had much to say as well about people who feign piety for their own purposes. He scathingly reprimanded the Pharisees for doing so by comparing them to whited tombs:

Woe unto you, scribes and Pharisees, hypocrites! For ye are like whited sepulchers, which indeed appear beautiful outward, but are within full of dead men's bones, and of all uncleanness. Even so ye also outwardly appear righteous unto men, but within ye are full of hypocrisy and iniquity (Mt. 23:27–28).

These men falsely professed faith while exploiting the true people of God. Compounding the tragedy, however, is the realization that they themselves could have been redeemed. Christ, in fact, died for them as well as for those who turned to Him by faith and found eternal life. The Scripture says that God

will have all men to be saved, and to come unto the knowledge of the truth. For there is one God, and one mediator between God and men, the man, Christ Jesus, Who gave himself a ransom for all, to be testified in due time (1 Tim. 2:4–6).

As the passage clearly indicates, the Lord would have *all* to be saved, having sent his Son to pay the purchase price of redemption for every human being. Yet false teachers make a calculated decision to deny the Lord and reject His free gift of eternal life. To make matters much worse, not only do they condemn themselves, but they lead countless masses of people to perdition with them. "And many," we are told, "shall follow their pernicious ways" (2:2).

Additionally, the Bible says that because of their blatant disregard for the truth and their indulgence in lifestyles that contradict virtually every aspect of godly living, "the way of truth shall be evil spoken of" (2:2). Such is the tragic legacy of false teachers. As we examine the details of their profligate conduct and doctrine, we shall discover precisely how they trample the truth and assassinate the credibility of the church.

IDENTIFYING MARKS

The apostle Peter delineates the central attributes of end-times false teachers. Although additional characteristics also come into play, their lives basically reflect four dominating features.

1. Lies. False teachers are masters of prevarication. They are deliberately loose with the truth, trading in "feigned words" (2:3). In other words, they are adroit and chronic liars.

2. Lucre. Not only do they lie, they strive to profit from their lies. Their willingness to market deception, to "make merchandise" (2:3), sets the stage for another serious problem—the exploitation of innocent people for gain. Like Balaam, they sell themselves for money.

3. Leisure. Their objective is to create lifestyles that totally contradict what Scripture commends in true men and women of God. It is said of them that they "count it pleasure to revel in the daytime" (2:13). The love of lucre and leisure become their obsessive addictions.

4. Lust. The final mark is their degeneration into lives of lust and self-indulgence, "having eyes full of adultery and that cannot cease from sin" (2:14). This deplorable condition becomes such a constant state of affairs that they are tragically described as "cursed children" (2:14).

The contrast between charlatans (chapter 2) and believers (chapter 1) is truly fascinating. While false teachers wallow in degradation on their path to eternal condemnation, believers are growing in grace on the way to spiritual maturity and eternal blessing. With false teachers, the process is not a progression but a digression. Theirs is the way down, while believers are on the way up. Thus the contrast between chapters 1 and 2 is indeed stark and foreboding because the onslaught of false teaching and dissolute conduct produced by such militant opposition to the truth will, in the end, help usher the world into its darkest hours.

CONCLUSION

The light of God's Word shining in dark places touches an extremely important issue in the lives and ministries of believers. As people trust Christ as their personal Savior, they become children of the light. Every child of God is placed in his or her sphere of influence as a light to the lost. When we commission missionaries and send them into remote areas of the world, we are placing lights in dark places—places where we may be unable to go ourselves.

As believers, we must exercise vigilance regarding the type of preaching and teaching we expose ourselves to. Unfortunately, we are plagued by people in both the pulpit and the media who make spectacular, dogmatic, and often entertaining claims to have received direct revelation from God. In many instances, they preach dramatically and influentially to huge throngs of people. But the fact remains that God has spoken definitively and with finality in the Scriptures. They alone are our source of divine revelation.

Balaam desired to "assist" the Lord in chastising His disobedient people. Of course, he really wanted what was in it for himself. We should keep in mind that God does not need our help to take His children to task. He didn't need it to correct Israel and the Jewish people, and He doesn't need it to correct our friends or those within our church fellowship.

FALLEN ANGELS AND 6
DROWNING MEN

The LORD knoweth how to deliver the godly out of temptations, and to reserve the unjust unto the day of judgment to be punished (2:9).

Judgment is a subject we seldom touch on these days. Instead, many contemporary Christians often tout their pride in being nonjudgmental as though it were a badge of honor. Although we should all desire to maintain a high standard of civility and good taste in our relationships with others, judgment is an inescapable reality. Never for a moment did Jesus, the prophets, or the penmen of the New Testament hesitate when they needed to issue solemn warnings on the topic. Peter's Epistles are no exception:

> *And through covetousness shall they, with feigned words, make merchandise of you; whose judgment now for a long time lingereth not, and their destruction slumbereth not (2:3).*

The verses that follow this declaration of impending judgment show a glaring contrast between the faithful and the faithless. Earlier Peter explains that, through the work of Christ within them, obedient believers can lead fulfilled and productive lives. And when the time comes to experience their exodus from this life, they are assured an abundant entrance into the presence of their waiting Lord. So the life of the trusting child of God is one of peace, assurance, and the anticipation that the best is yet to come.

In contrast to this constructive life pattern are the pronouncements of judgment and perdition that God heaps on those who pervert the truth. Long ago He promised to execute His wrath on people who exploit believers "with false words." In Deuteronomy 32:35 we find these words:

> *To me belongeth vengeance, and recompense; their foot shall slide in due time. For the day of their calamity is at hand, and the things that shall come upon them make haste.*

The words *in due time* are instructive. Although individuals who traffic in error and deceit appear to have a present advantage, their position is only temporary. The idea in this verse is that their destruction is not asleep. God is not napping while they reap benefits for propagating and practicing iniquity. He warns those who consistently enjoy sin that their prosperity will only last a season. Then comes the winter.

NO BETTER THAN THE ANGELS

The consequences false teachers face as a result of their promiscuous folly is no light matter. Peter cites three instances where God meted out severe and definitive judgment. First, the Holy Spirit calls to mind the angels who followed Satan and fell into an irreparable condition:

> *For if God spared not the angels that sinned,*
> *but cast them down to hell, and delivered them*
> *into chains of darkness, to be reserved unto*
> *judgment . . . (2:4).*

The force of this statement lies in its demand for an answer. It might be phrased this way:

"Do you think for a minute that you are any better than the angels who fell? They have been cast down to hell and await their turn to stand before the bar of God's eternal judgment and wrath."

In light of this fact, it would be a monumental miscalculation to believe that, if God dealt this severely with angelic beings, man could escape.

Jude 6 tells us a bit more about these fallen angels:

> *And the angels who kept not their first estate, but*
> *left their own habitation, he hath reserved in ever-*
> *lasting chains under darkness unto the judgment*
> *of the great day.*

These angels are identified as those who joined Satan in the great rebellion against God, spoken of in Isaiah 14:12–17. Verses 13–14 cut to the heart of the matter:

> *For thou [Satan] hast said in thine heart, I will ascend*
> *into heaven, I will exalt my throne above the stars of*
> *God; I will sit also upon the mount of the congrega-*
> *tion, in the sides of the north, I will ascend above the*
> *heights of the clouds, I will be like the Most High.*

The repetition of the first-person pronoun *I* appears no fewer than five times in two verses and strikes to the very heart of Satan's problem. It reveals an insatiable pride in self that spawns innumerable manifestations of evil. Among the foremost is an obsession to wrest from God the glory that is His alone. If Satan could accomplish this feat, he could establish his evil dominion over all that God has created. The former "covering Cherub" would then become "like the Most High." In other words, Satan would depose the Creator and become God.

Following the tracks of the great deceiver across the pages of the prophetic Scriptures confirms what we have seen here. The Antichrist, Satan's counterfeit to the true Christ, will enter the Temple in Jerusalem during the future Tribulation period and will declare himself to be God (2 Th. 2:4). Then the world finally will see the visible proof of Satan's ambitions as stated in Isaiah 14, written more than 2,700 years ago. The vile taproot from which all evil desire and design spring is pride. Is it any wonder that Jehovah genuinely hates pride?

> *The fear of the* LORD *is to hate evil; pride, and arrogance, and the evil way, and the perverse mouth, do I hate* (Prov. 8:13).

Some people, no doubt, question the Lord's motives in warning His creatures to steer clear of pride. He does so not because He Himself personifies pride and will not abide competition but rather, to the contrary. Of course, we know that the one true God, as Creator and Supreme Ruler of the universe, is alone the rightful recipient of glory, praise, and honor. And we worship Him thus. The reason He so persistently warns us against falling prey to pride is that He fully understands the devastating effect it has on us. Consequently, He carefully allows us to witness its consequences without tasting for ourselves the pain that pride can bring.

These false teachers provide some of the best examples of pride that are found in the Word. Their entire system is built on the folly of this great sin. They see themselves as the center of the universe. As a result, they willfully rebel against God, mutilate His people through deception and exploitation, and cause the lost to stumble into hell. In this respect, they are no different than their true master, the Devil. And, as we have seen, they share a full measure of his condemnation.

When hosts of angels followed Lucifer in his great rebellion against God, they were guilty of joining the arch deceiver. Admittedly, this event is one of the premier mysteries in the universe. Why such enlightened beings would choose to follow the supreme practitioner of lies and deceit remains a question without a satisfactory answer. But, in a demonstrably terminal way, they did; and we live with the results every day of our lives. It is a phenomenon more easily observed than explained. It also raises another question, which is nearly as mysterious.

Why do human beings who otherwise seem rational and stable blindly follow maniacal false teachers? For instance, why would an entire nation allow itself to become mesmerized by Adolph Hitler? The man was a devotee of the occult who wantonly slaughtered millions of innocent people and devastated the whole of Europe. Or why would more than 900 individuals line up in the jungles of Guyana in 1978 and drink powdered juice mixed with cyanide on orders from Jim Jones, a deeply disturbed cultist? We might also ask ourselves why so many were captivated by the likes of David Koresh. The Branch Davidian leader was no more than a scruffy ranter with messianic delusions who convinced his followers to follow him to death by fire in 1993 in Waco, Texas.

In these and like instances, there are no totally satisfactory answers, only a fact to be recognized: Some people are willing to follow, even if it means their own destruction.

Given to Godlessness

> *And spared not the old world, but saved Noah, the eighth person, a preacher of righteousness, bringing in the flood upon the world of the ungodly* (2:5).

Peter's second example is the case of those who perished in the flood in the days of Noah. Here there is a different twist. The emphasis is not as much on whom they followed but on whose preaching they resisted. Hebrews 11:7 succinctly describes the ministry of Noah:

> *By faith Noah, being warned of God of things not seen yet, moved with fear, prepared an ark to the saving of his house, by which he condemned the world, and became heir of the righteousness which is by faith.*

Noah, "a preacher of righteousness," by word and deed, bore a testimony that spoke clearly of the impending doom of a world wholly given to godlessness. But those who heard him and saw the preparation of the ark still refused to believe. Theirs was a deliberate decision to conduct business as usual and live self-indulgent, godless lives. Consequently, they perished in the universal flood. The depths to which humanity had fallen is recorded in Genesis 6:5:

> *And God saw that the wickedness of man was great in the earth, and that every imagination of the thoughts of his heart was only evil continually.*

It would be a good idea for mankind to learn from the past and not repeat the folly of Noah's contemporaries. Obviously, however, such has not been the case. The men and women of this generation have rejected the Word of God and the messages of modern preachers of

righteousness just as clearly as did the people of old.
And they have done so despite prodigious warning of
the consequences. Jesus Himself described these consequences in the most descriptive terms:

> But as the days of Noah were, so shall also the com-
> ing of the Son of Man be. For as in the days that
> were before the flood they were eating and drinking,
> marrying and giving in marriage, until the day
> that Noah entered into the ark, And knew not until
> the flood came, and took them all away, so shall also
> the coming of the Son of man be. Then shall two be
> in the field; the one shall be taken, and the other left.
> Two women shall be grinding at the mill; the one
> shall be taken, and the other left (Mt. 24:37–41).

Most of us are familiar with the words of the American
philosopher George Santayana, who said, "Those who cannot remember the past are condemned to repeat it."
Unfortunately, the story of humanity abounds with tragic
chronicles that illustrate the price societies have paid for
failing to heed history. The failures of end-times generations may well be related predominantly to their repudiation of the Word of God. This grave fault dooms societies to
repeat, often in worse fashion, the errors of the past.

As it was in the days of Noah, so it is in our day. A corrupt
secular society repudiates the Scriptures while patting itself
on the back for being "politically correct." It fights all
attempts to display the revered Ten Commandments in
classrooms and public buildings and decries all moral decen-
cy and order as set forth in the Word of God. Unfortunately,
these public outcries have so intimidated many government
officials that they have forfeited their God-ordained obliga-
tion to promote morality and maintain order.

A companion manifestation to rejecting divine revelation is to react against those who proclaim and teach it. Noah's words were scorned to the point of ridicule. After spending more than 100 years warning people about what was ahead, he could claim only the members of his immediate family as beneficiaries of divine grace. Today we are witnessing a similar turn of events. Conscientious, conservative Christians and their ministers are being regarded as society's undesirable elements. Increasingly, they are being subjected to ridicule, resentment, and reactionary attitudes. Yet only a few years ago, they would have been considered our model citizens.

In Matthew 24, Jesus tells us what lies ahead for a generation condemned to repeat what it has refused to learn. The people who are taken away—the one "in the field" and the other "grinding at the mill"—are not being swept up to heaven in the Rapture, as some teach. Quite the contrary. They are taken away to judgment, as they were in the time of Noah. We can hardly overstate the severity of the wrath God will execute on unbelievers and their false teachers. It is far better to learn the lessons of Noah's day than to relive its tragedies.

When Nothing Is Left but Judgment

The third example of the condemnation false teachers bring down on their own heads is found in the record of the ancient cities of Sodom and Gomorrah:

> *And, turning the cities of Sodom and Gomorrah into ashes, condemned them with an overthrow, making them an example unto those that after should live ungodly* (2:6).

These twin cities serve as a window into what transpires when truth is repudiated and evil is so unreservedly tolerated and embraced that it becomes encoded as a community lifestyle standard. The progressive degradation, which ends with the cataclysmic judgment found in 2 Peter, parallels the process found in Romans 1.

Romans records the course disintegrating societies embrace in their descent to national oblivion and divine judgment. The first step involves repudiating God to follow other masters:

> Because, when they knew God, they glorified him
> not as God, neither were thankful, but became
> vain in their imaginations, and their foolish heart
> was darkened (Rom. 1:21).

Next is the denial of truth. This step, of course, implies deliberate rejection of both the message and the messengers of divine revelation:

> Who exchanged the truth of God for a lie, and wor-
> shiped and served the creature more than the
> Creator, who is blessed forever. Amen (Rom. 1:25).

When man has fully assimilated Satan's big lie, he comes to believe that he has actually become like God. It then follows that he regards his creature-oriented environment as bearing divine distinctives. And so he falls prey to the ultimate form of destructive idolatry—creature worship.

Devoid of the compass of biblical truth or teachers of biblical spirituality, humanity shifts to a standard where anything goes. Whatever the degenerate mind of man can conceive is accepted and promoted as right and good. Following a bewildering downward spiral, virtually every previously accepted norm is violated and socio-religious and political order is destroyed. Inherent in the process, perhaps the bottom rung on this ladder to hell, is the annihilation of the family. Family, after all, is the most fundamental element in organized society. Society, as we have known it in the Western world, cannot function successfully without the cohesive properties emanating from the structured family unit.

According to what Romans conveys, the epitome of dysfunctional society comes with the introduction of same-sex relationships:

> And likewise also the men, leaving the natural use of the woman, burned in their lust toward one another, men with men working that which is unseemly, and receiving in themselves that recompense of their error which was fitting (Rom. 1:27).

All of this serves to bring us back to Sodom and Gomorrah. For what we witness in the destruction of these ancient cities seems to mirror the final consequences of the transgressions listed in Romans and corresponding passages when there is no alternative to judgment. The destruction of Sodom and Gomorrah is recorded in the book of Genesis, chapters 18 and 19. Several important factors immediately confront us.

Abraham received a visit from three heavenly personages. Two were angels; the other was none other than the Lord Himself: "And the LORD appeared unto him by the oaks of Mamre: and he sat in the tent door in the heat of the day" (Gen. 18:1). This preincarnate appearance of Christ was important for at least two reasons. First, He came to reveal to Abraham that, in spite of her advanced age, "Sarah, thy wife, shall have a son" (Gen. 18:10). This announcement would shape the entire future of God's dealing with mankind in mercy and grace. Next, He declared the execution of God's wrath on godless society. Therefore, the Lord was magnifying His mercy and manifesting His wrath at the same time.

In the course of Abraham's intercession for the godly remnant he believed to be in Sodom and Gomorrah, he asked a question that has been repeated for millennia: "Shall not the Judge of all the earth do right?" (Gen. 18:25).

The response provides an awe-inspiring view of essential divine attributes. The God of all the earth will indeed do right. He will extend grace and mercy to unworthy sinners through the redeeming work of the Messiah. But He also will execute judgment on those who willfully reject His grace and violate the precepts for orderly society. In other words, we have a clear illustration that there is indeed a heaven to be gained and a hell to be shunned. Today, when wickedness is often concealed by a false view of God's love, it would behoove us to learn this lesson.

A RESPECT FOR REMNANTS

Abraham's intercession and the Lord's reaction exhibit an important principle:

Suppose there are fifty righteous within the city:
wilt thou also destroy and not spare the place for
the fifty righteous that are in it? (Gen. 18:24).

The Lord answered that He would not destroy the city if fifty righteous people lived there. The numbers diminished until the patriarch was pleading for only ten righteous. Yet the Lord's answer was the same. He promised to spare Sodom if as few as ten righteous people could be found there.

Since the fall of man, the godly have always been a minority of the population. In this day of grace, the Lord is careful to show us the same principle He demonstrated to Abraham. Ephesians 2 speaks of two remnants being called out by God. One is a remnant from among the Jewish people. The other is a remnant from among the Gentiles. The church, therefore, is neither an extension of Judaism nor a Gentile institution. These remnants constitute a unique body—His body. And within that body dwells the presence of God in the person of the Holy Spirit. These remnants function as a witness from the Lord to the nations, inviting individuals to receive, through the gospel, eternal life.

As implied in the Genesis account, a godly remnant also acts as a preserving agent, retarding the execution of deserved judgment. Of course, the world neither recognizes nor respects this fact. Indeed, the very opposite is true. For when Lot pleaded with the men of Sodom to stop their lustful pursuit of the two angels, they soundly rebuked him:

> And they said, Stand back. And they said again, This one fellow came in to sojourn, and he will needs be a judge: now will we deal worse with thee, than with them. And they pressed hard against the man, even Lot, and came near to break the door (Gen. 19:9).

Lot apparently had risen to some stature in Sodom. It is revealing to read what Scripture has to say about this man, who is often projected as a dissolute individual.

> And [God] delivered just [righteous] Lot, vexed with the filthy manner of life of the wicked (For that righteous man dwelling among them, in seeing and hearing, vexed his righteous soul from day to day with their unlawful deeds) (2:7–8).

Lot may have been among them, but he was not like them. Lot had sullied his character, so that he was less than a sterling example of belief in Jehovah. Nevertheless, he was still a true believer; and God treated him accordingly.

GIVING THE DEVIL HIS DUE

God's wrath, which was poured out on Sodom and Gomorrah, demonstrates what happens when unbridled evil runs its course.

First comes a refusal to give God the deference due Him. This step is followed by man's exaltation of himself as the center of the universe. The inevitable consequence is man's complete repudiation of divine, spiritual, and moral norms. The process bottoms out when evil takes over, and the substance of life consists of the pursuit of lust and self-gratification.

Perhaps the defining word for the entire scenario is given to us in Genesis 19:11:

And they [the angels] smote the men that were at the door of the house with blindness, both small and great; so that they wearied themselves to find the door.

Blindness is the operative word. Consumed by their homosexual lust, these men were blind to their sin. Their conduct was perfectly acceptable to them—so much so, in fact, that being smitten with blindness and confusion still did not quell their passion. Sodom and Gomorrah had hit rock bottom, and they would pay dearly for their transgressions.

What happened in Sodom that dreadful day is indicative of the downward spiral to judgment and wrath experienced by every society, small or great, that chooses to follow a similar course of action. The account, therefore, speaks loudly to us. We can measure approximately where our society fits on the scale of holiness by looking at the evil we embrace and enshrine on the one hand and the righteousness we scorn and repudiate on the other.

Time and again, people fail to recognize that there is a fatal price to pay for walking away from God. Perhaps the reason for this blindness is that, by the time people begin to reap what they have sown, they are so biblically illiterate they wouldn't know the truth if they heard it. There is an extremely dark side to all this. The time comes when the cup of iniquity is full—when God says, "That's enough." One of the most ominous statements in Scripture is found in Romans 1:28: "And even as they did not like to retain God in their knowledge, God gave them over to a reprobate mind."

The time indeed comes when wicked societies arrive at a juncture where there is no turning back. Their situation becomes irreparable. Judgment becomes the only alternative.

Liberal theologians and assorted other skeptics have often derided the Old Testament as a "bloody book," unworthy of propagation in "enlightened cultures" such as ours. These dissenters regard God's treatment of the Canaanites and other ancient peoples as cruel and unusual punishment. However, when we study ancient history objectively, we learn that these cultures had become so degenerate and corrupt that their very existence was a threat to their contemporaries.

With respect to their relationship to Israel, this fact is particularly relevant. God's purpose for the children of Abraham was to bring potential blessing to the whole of humanity through the Messiah. Thus the Israelites needed to have zero tolerance for degenerate moral and spiritual practices. But when people view the transgressors as somehow more worthy of sympathy and consideration than those transgressed against, the social order suffers the consequences.

Sodom and Gomorrah are prime illustrations. They were so thoroughly given over to wickedness that no reason remained for them to continue to disgrace themselves and pollute the region.

> Then the LORD rained upon Sodom and upon Gomorrah brimstone and fire from the LORD out of heaven; And he overthrew those cities, and all the plain, and all the inhabitants of the cities, and that which grew upon the ground (Gen. 19:24–25).

Shall not the Judge of all the earth do right? He did. And we can all be thankful.

A SILVER LINING

We know the phrase well. "Every cloud must have a silver lining." Anyone immersed in trauma probably would take issue with such a cheery outlook, but it is a rather good observation. Good, that is, for believers. For those of us surrounded by the spiritual chaos created by false teachers, we have a good word—a silver lining. It is really the best news to come from an otherwise somber narrative. But first comes a stern warning.

The wrath God poured out on Sodom and Gomorrah should be held up as a deterrent for those who might choose to follow these cities' iniquitous path:

> And, turning the cities of Sodom and Gomorrah into ashes, [God] condemned them with an overthrow, making them an example unto those that after should live ungodly (2:6).

Perhaps the lost seldom learn. Nevertheless, God provides a word to all who will heed it: "Don't do what they did!"

His good news for believers is the antithesis of the despair reserved for the ungodly.

> *The Lord knoweth how to deliver the godly out of temptations, and to reserve the unjust unto the day of judgment to be punished* (2:9).

Lot and his immediate family testify to this Word. They were "delivered" from the all-consuming fires of judgment even though the angels literally had to drag them out of Sodom by the hand. Nonetheless, they were delivered.

And so will we be too. Before the fires of the Tribulation period descend, the Lord will rapture the church and take His beloved Bride to Himself. Some, like Lot, may make a rather reluctant exit. But exit they will.

A friend of mine once related a conversation he had had on the subject with a wealthy Christian friend from California. "When the Rapture takes place," he told his friend, "God will have to take you kicking and screaming. You have come to love your toys so much that it will grieve you to leave them behind."

For Americans, that picture may accurately reflect how fondly some of us have embraced the "toys" of our affluent culture. But our situations will change in an instant.

> *As it is written, Eye hath not seen, nor ear heard, neither have entered into the heart of man, the things which God hath prepared for them that love him* (1 Cor. 2:9).

This verse speaks to the marvelous revelation He has given us through the "knowledge of him that hath called us to glory and virtue" (1:3). But included in that knowledge are the wonders of what He is preparing for us. And when we experience that twinkling-of-an-eye departure from this planet, the shabby spoils of this life will fade like shadows before the brilliance of the sun.

Meanwhile, we have a storehouse of daily deliverance to draw from while here on Earth. As the apostle Paul wrote,

> There hath no temptation taken you but such as is common to man; but God is faithful, who will not permit you to be tempted above that ye are able, but will, with the temptation, also make the way to escape, that ye may be able to bear it (1 Cor. 10:13).

Whether it be a solicitation to do evil or the weight of a severe trial, temptation is the common affliction of us all. English novelist Margaret Oliphant once observed, "Temptations come, as a general rule, when they are sought." We may succumb because we fail to truly seek the way out that God has provided.

Lot's deliverance from Sodom came at the hands of the angels who led him from the city. Our deliverer is none other than the Lord Himself. Hebrews states so in compelling terms:

> For in that he himself hath suffered being tempted, he is able to help them that are tempted (Heb. 2:18).

When Jesus chose to mantel His glory in human flesh, He appropriated a full measure of the human experience. He endured temptation as we do. Yet He suffered through those dreadful times and tells us today that He not only under-stands but extends to us His mighty hand of deliverance:

> For we have not an high priest who cannot be touched with the feeling of our infirmities, but was in all points tempted like as we are, yet without sin. Let us, therefore, come boldly unto the throne of grace, that we may obtain mercy, and find grace to help in time of need (Heb. 4:15–16).

CONCLUSION

God allows temptation into our lives so that He can bring us through it, not because He plans to leave us in it. Lot was not abandoned in Sodom. He was led through and brought out. Such is the pattern for deliverance. Adversity, temptations, and trials enable us to experience, in a deeper way, the all-sufficiency of Christ. Thus we grow and move toward maturity.

WELLS WITHOUT WATER, CLOUDS WITH NO RAIN 7

These are wells without water, clouds that are carried with a tempest, to whom the mist of darkness is reserved forever (2:17).

False teachers have nothing to offer except spiritual drought and darkness. The barrenness of these men and their teachings are delineated from verses 10 through 18 of chapter 2. There the Holy Spirit exposes their basic character traits, their true attitudes toward God and His dominion, and the depth of their animosity:

> But chiefly them that walk after the flesh in the lust of uncleanness, and despise government. Presumptuous are they; self-willed, they are not afraid to speak evil of dignities (2:10).

False teachers and fallen angels are of a common lot. They are unrestrained in their blasphemous disrespect for the government of God and are not in the least hesitant to revile the highest of angelic authorities. In spirit, they are like the greatest of all fallen angels, Satan himself, who does not fear even to show his contempt for God while in the very presence of the Most High.

We see that contempt in the book of Job. Job was a man who was upright, God-fearing, and a portrait of what it means to be righteous. When the Lord pointed out these godly attributes to Satan, the evil one responded,

> Doth Job fear God for nothing? But put forth thine hand now, and touch all that he hath, and he will curse thee to thy face (1:9, 11).

Such unfeigned arrogance unmasks the true character of the wily "angel of light."

The conduct of the coming Antichrist also furnishes a good illustration with regard to the disrespect evidenced toward God, His people, and His government:

> And he opened his mouth in blasphemy against God, to blaspheme his name, and his tabernacle, and them that dwell in heaven (Rev. 13:6).

Here is a prime example of the attitudes of the totally self-absorbed. Their lives completely revolve around the credo "anything by any means for me and mine."

We often hear about the "Me" generation. The expression superbly catches the spirit of a satanically driven age that is increasingly devoid of reverence for God and established authority. It is little wonder that we hear so many stories about people who commit the most heinous crimes, believing they have a right to take whatever it is they want. After all, aren't they the center and circumference of life? To such people, nothing but their own pleasure and self-indulgence are of any consequence.

More insidious and pervasive still is the virtually total disrespect for the name of God in modern society. Scripture reveals that a chief characteristic of Satan and his Antichrist is blasphemy (Rev. 13:5–6). When we hear the Lord's name defamed without rebuke throughout society, from the news media down to the youngest of children, we can understand just how deep the gathering darkness is becoming. But the question is, What do we do about it? Perhaps we have a helpful hint in the conduct of unfallen angels.

WHERE ANGELS FEAR TO TREAD

Whereas angels, who are greater in power and might, bring not railing accusation against them before the Lord (2:11).

Although false teachers do not hesitate to rail against angels, going even as far, perhaps, as to question their very existence, the angels do not respond in kind. Instead, they leave the matter to the Lord. No doubt, the angels are well aware that God has all things well in hand; and they can leave the situation with Him.

But where should we as believers draw the line in reacting to charlatans and frauds and leveling attacks against them? It may well be that we must differentiate between the personalities and the falsehoods they propagate.

When I first became a Christian and tried to witness to the people I worked with, I immediately ran into severe testing. About all I knew at that point was that I was saved. One older man who attended a liberal church in our community made it his business to make life difficult for me. He often ridiculed my faith and asked questions I was not equipped to answer. Sometimes he even got the other fellows on our crew laughing with him and pressing the issue, all at my expense. Finally I came to the end of my tether. I decided to make myself feel better by making him feel much worse.

One day I sat in my little cubicle having lunch and, as I had been advised to do, was reading the New Testament. I no longer put much stock in the Bible-reading method of those days, when I used to close my eyes, let the Word of God fall open, then place my finger somewhere on the page, expecting some great revelation. But this time, perhaps because the Lord pitied my ignorance and immaturity, He graciously provided help. There on the page before me lay these words:

> *Dearly beloved, avenge not yourselves but, rather,*
> *give place unto wrath; for it is written, Vengeance*
> *is mine; I will repay, saith the Lord* (Rom. 12:19).

It was good advice for a new Christian. And over the years, God has shown me repeatedly that it is still good advice. The Lord is perfectly capable of taking care of our adversaries.

If we attempt to react to every attack launched by some noxious personality, we become distracted from the central purpose of our lives and run the risk of giving our opponents much more attention than they warrant. One point is certain: when we expend our energy exposing charlatans, frauds, or people who are just downright malicious, we seldom really win. The Devil has a long line of successors waiting in the wings. He never runs out of agitators, deceivers, or individuals who thrive at the expense of the sincere and godly.

However, it may be one thing to restrain ourselves from retaliating against personal attacks but quite another to shrink from upholding the truth. When it comes to being guardians of the truth, we are instructed to contend for the faith:

And exhort you that ye should earnestly contend for the faith which was once delivered unto the saints. For there are certain men crept in unawares, who were before of old ordained to this condemnation, ungodly men, turning the grace of our God into lasciviousness, and denying the only Lord God, and our Lord Jesus Christ (Jude 3–4).

In this passage, contending for the faith involves the central issues of the gospel related to the grace of God and the person of the Lord Jesus Christ. False teaching in these areas should never go unchallenged. The persistent proclamation of the truth is the abiding antidote for deceitful teachers and their fellow travelers.

THE REWARD OF UNRIGHTEOUSNESS

Just as believers are assured of a reward for their faithful service for Christ in this world (1 Cor. 3), the emissaries of Satan also are guaranteed that they, too, have a "reward" awaiting them:

But these, as natural brute beasts, made to be taken and destroyed, speak evil of the things that they understand not, and shall utterly perish in their own corruption (2:12).

These words are strikingly similar to those in Jeremiah 12:3. False teachers were plaguing the prophet, who was deeply perplexed by their hatred for him and his message. These men came from the priestly town of Anathoth, Jeremiah's hometown; and they went so far as to demand that he cease speaking in God's name. They even wanted to kill him. Like false teachers in every era, the men of Anathoth spoke often of God and His favor toward them.

Yet, in actuality, they did not know Him, for Jeremiah would exclaim: "Thou [God] art near their mouth, and far from their heart" (Jer. 12:2). "Why," he wondered, "doth the way of the wicked prosper? Why are all they happy that deal very treacherously?" (Jer. 12:1).

Jeremiah could not fathom why these men, who were so far from God, appeared to be reaping the abundance of His blessing. He was suffering, yet they were prospering. He simply could not understand it. But God would have the last word. And like the unbelievers in Jesus' parable of the wheat and the tares, these false prophets would be allowed to grow with the true people of God until the harvest came. Then, however, the Lord would pluck them out (Mt. 13:24–30):

> I will punish them. . . .And there shall be no remnant of them; for I will bring evil upon the men of Anathoth, even the year of their judgment. . . . Pull them out like sheep for the slaughter, and prepare them for the day of slaughter" (Jer. 11:22–23; 12:3).

These words are extremely strong, and we do well to remember them. Eventually God will destroy the false teachers. They shall "utterly perish" (2:12). The short run is immaterial. In the long run, no matter how prosperous they may appear at the moment, they are headed for disaster. The more pressing problem is whom they will deceive and take with them.

In all of this, we can learn to apply the Gamaliel principle. Gamaliel was a revered teacher in Israel in the days of the early church. He was the man who had taught Saul, who later became the apostle Paul. When Israel's ruling body, the Sanhedrin, convened to decide what to do about the men who were preaching Christ, he advised them against taking harsh action:

> And now I say unto you, Refrain from these men, and let them alone; for if this counsel or this work be of men, it will come to nothing; But if it be of God, ye cannot overthrow it, lest perhaps ye be found even to fight against God (Acts 5:38–39).

SPOTS AND BLEMISHES

> And [they] shall receive the reward of unright-eousness, as they that count it pleasure to revel in the daytime. Spots they are and blemishes, revel-ing with their own deceivings while they feast with you (2:13).

Calling false teachers "spots" and "blemishes" graphically describes the reality of their chosen lifestyle. The language emphasizes their abandonment to licentious living. It seems there may well be two aspects to this phase of their lives.

The first aspect concerns the visible: they openly flaunt their revelry and self-indulgence. In Peter's day, they carried this obsession so far that they even turned Christian celebrations into riotous drinking parties and tried to conceal their promiscuity with pious protestations of devotion to God. They remind us of the scribes and Pharisees who opposed the Lord Jesus. Jesus not only exposed them for what they were but condemned them and pronounced their final destruction.

The second aspect concerns the invisible—the inner, unseen man.

> *Having eyes full of adultery and that cannot cease from sin; beguiling unstable souls; an heart they have exercised with covetous practices; cursed children* (2:14).

Beyond their obsession with licentious living, they were consumed with lust for sensual passion and possessions. Although their followers saw them as great paragons of piety with a practical twist, God saw them as "cursed children."

It seems strange indeed that such obvious evil can be passed off as acceptable to God. But it happens frequently. In our lifetime, we have witnessed some of the worst immoral debauchery cloaked with religious manipulation. Some false teachers have even been catapulted to messianic heights by their deluded followers.

Of course, people do what they do because they are what they are. Verse 22 makes this case with exceptionally vivid imagery:

> *But it is happened unto them according to the true proverb, The dog is turned to his own vomit again; and the sow that was washed, to her wallowing in the mire.*

TELLING IT AS IT IS

Before closing the book on false teachers for "whom the mist of darkness is reserved forever" (2:17), Peter exposes the carnage their spiritual profligacy leaves behind. The devastation is immense. In every sense, these frauds are "wells without water" and clouds with no rain. What a contrast between the fruit they bear and that of the Lord

Jesus. When Jesus says, "If any man thirst, let him come unto me, and drink" (Jn. 7:37), He offers eternal substance and sustenance. Two thousand years later we see this truth exhibited in the lives of millions of believers worldwide. But false teachers come and go, and the spiritual thirst of their followers is never sated:

> *For when they speak great swelling words of vanity, they allure through the lusts of the flesh, through much wantonness, those that are just escaping from them who live in error* (2:18).

False teachers specialize in rhetoric without spiritual reality. They speak deftly, with great authority; but their words simply meander vainly. They major in snaring people who are not grounded in spiritual truth. In Peter's day, many people who were "just escaping from them who live in error" were being seduced by these men. The emphasis here probably best fits those who, through association with Christians, were beginning to break away from their pagan practices. Tragically, although they were moving toward the truth, they were encouraged to return to the lusts that they had started to abandon.

The barefaced abandonment to perverse practices that we read of here is somewhat mystifying. Even more astonishing, however, is that people, even today, flock in record numbers to such obvious purveyors of error, who appeal strictly to the flesh and its baser proclivities.

The men Peter refers to actually were propagating antinomianism. They taught that once people made a profession of faith in Christ, anything they did in the flesh, particularly in sexual matters, was of no consequence. Antinomians went so far as to say that the more one sinned, the greater the magnitude of grace God displayed in furnishing forgiveness. According to such thinking, sinful behavior is not that bad. In fact, it even appears to have a beneficial aspect.

Such false teachers were experts in telling people what they wanted to hear. That was the spirit of their activities in Peter's day; and, sad to say, it is rapidly becoming the spirit of the age in which we live.

When the baby boomers of the 1960s decided to try attending church, they created a dilemma for many evangelicals. These children of the "Me" generation had tired of their toys and were disappointed to find that possessions were not enough to hold their families together and provide personal peace. So they decided to give the church a chance.

But these individuals had not been reared in the Judeo-Christian environment of former generations. They had long since succumbed to the hedonistic gibberish of secular professors, pop psychologists, and the pagan icons of their contemporary culture. Author Harry F. Waters has described these people as "designed and manufactured for the video generation."

So there ensued a conflict of perceptions. The baby boomers were seeking solace for their needs, *as they perceived them*. Their greatest need, however, as perceived by biblical evangelicals, was for the gospel. But the message of repentance and faith in Christ was foreign and often odious to these neopagans. They wanted order and meaning for their lives and those of their children.

Would churches straightforwardly and boldly present Christ and then deal with the growth needs of truly saved baby boomers? Or would they opt for feeding these lost souls what they wanted and hope that salvation would come by osmosis at some point down the line? The answer is obvious: Some would; some would not. Consequently, we have today a plethora of churches oriented more toward offering entertainment and "how-to" programs, rather than enlightenment in the things of God.

The result is a culture that tends toward the "I'm okay, you're okay" mentality and embraces, in a professedly nonjudgmental way, various religious systems that disdain and even deny fundamental aspects of biblical Christianity. Believers who obey God's mandate to make Christ known to everyone everywhere are becoming increasingly isolated. If you believe that people without Christ are lost and need salvation, you not only are ridiculed as intolerant but are now described as a promoter of hatred and divisiveness. The future on Earth doesn't look good for those of us who refuse to compromise the true message of Scripture.

> *While they promise them liberty, they themselves are the servants of corruption; for of whom a man is overcome, of the same is he brought in bondage* (2:19).

False teachers promise liberty through license. Their words echo those of the Devil in Genesis 3:

> *For God doth know that in the day ye eat thereof, then your eyes shall be opened, and ye shall be as God, knowing good and evil* (Gen. 3:5).

Satan's smooth words to Eve promised liberty. In reality, however, they brought corruption and servitude. Like our great adversary, false teachers even today promise liberty and freedom to those who follow their heretical teachings. Yet they themselves are not free. They are victims of their own apostate rebelliousness, which shackles them to their dark passions and consumes them with the desire to satisfy themselves.

The enslaving aspect of self-inflicted servitude was something even the pagans of Peter's day could understand. The Roman philosopher and teacher of Emperor Nero once said, "To be enslaved to oneself is the heaviest of all servitudes." These apostates had thoroughly embraced the allure of empty self-gratification.

The fruit they bore contrasts sharply with that of the Lord Jesus. He, too, made a promise. When He came to the synagogue in Nazareth, He used the Scripture to declare the legacy of the Messiah's ministry:

> And he came to Nazareth, where he had been brought up; and, as his custom was, he went into the synagogue on the sabbath day, and stood up to read. The Spirit of the Lord is upon me, because he hath anointed me to preach the gospel to the poor; he hath sent me to heal the brokenhearted, to preach deliverance to the captives, and recovering of sight to the blind, to set at liberty them that are bruised (Lk. 4:16, 18).

Our Lord delivered on that promise; and for 2,000 years, He has been setting captives free. That freedom liberates us from servitude to self and enables us to serve a higher Master—God and His Christ.

> For if, after they have escaped the pollutions of the world through the knowledge of the Lord and Savior, Jesus Christ, they are again entangled in it, and overcome, the latter end is worse with them than the beginning. For it had been better for them not to have known the way of righteousness than, after they have known it, to turn from the holy commandment delivered unto them (2:20–21).

False teachers are apostates. Bible scholar Dr. John Walvoord has described them as "people who outwardly claim to be Christians but actually have no Christian faith." In other words, they pretend to be what they are not. They are wolves in sheep's clothing.

No doubt, many people hear these pretenders speak in the name of God and Christ and wonder how unbelievers can preach and teach in His name, yet be children of darkness. The Lord puts this dilemma in perspective when He speaks of judgment and of those who will face the consequences of their deeds:

> Many will say to me in that day, Lord, Lord, have we not prophesied in thy name? And in thy name have cast out demons? And in thy name done many wonderful works? And then will I profess unto them, I never knew you; depart from me, ye that work iniquity (Mt. 7:22–23).

Evidently, the false teachers the apostle Peter referred to had made some outward profession of faith in the past. But, as in Jesus' parable of the seed and the sower, their hearts were like stony ground; and the seeds that fell did not endure:

> But he that received the seed in stony places, the same is he that heareth the word, and immediately with joy receiveth it; Yet hath he not root in himself, but endureth for a while; for when tribulation or persecution ariseth because of the word, immediately he is offended (Mt. 13:20–21).

For a person to hear the message of the gospel and reject it out of hand is a tragedy. But to reject the truth, then cynically choose to use a sacred office for personal profit by beguiling the unstable and immature, is a tragedy compounded a thousandfold. It would, indeed, be better if such people had not known the way of righteousness than to have turned from it. It would be better still had they never been born.

But beyond their self-inflicted condemnation lies a greater weight of accountability. False teachers ply their perversions at the expense of others. Over the millennia, these charlatans have victimized millions of souls and carried them down into the pit with them because of their deceitful doctrine of lies, lust, and self-indulgence. For the most part, the victims were potential believers who could have been directed toward the Lord instead of away from Him. Consequently, false teachers bear this tremendous weight of responsibility, and they will answer to God for what they have done. It is an awesome and somber prospect.

We can be sure that the aged apostle felt a great burden for the people who fell prey to men like these. He had been instructed by the Lord Jesus to "feed my lambs" and twice to "feed my sheep" (Jn. 21:15, 17). And he took this charge seriously. Peter realized that the flock belongs to Christ. As pastors, missionaries, teachers, and parents, we are but undershepherds. It is an overwhelming privilege and responsibility to be entrusted with caring for His people.

CONCLUSION

Like fake money printed on sophisticated presses, counterfeits are sometimes hard to spot. But no matter how genuine they may appear, they are still just counterfeits. In these last days, we must constantly guard against purveyors of religion without reality. Many people today are swept into cults because every cult or false religion appears sincere and seems to be doing some good work. We discern whether they are of the Lord, however, not by evaluating the good they may do but by inspecting their fidelity (or lack of it) to the Word of God and the person of Jesus Christ.

We can expose false teachers by holding them to the scriptural standards of conduct set for spiritual leaders. If we know what 2 Peter and companion passages say to us about the characteristics of such deceivers, we can be equipped to recognize them.

Finally, test a teacher by what or whom he promotes most zealously. Is it himself or the Savior? Remember that the ministry of the Holy Spirit is not to glorify Himself but to exalt the Son. The same should be true of all who are genuine men and women of God.

A LOOK AT
OUR FUTURE

Looking for and hasting unto the coming of the day of God, in which the heavens, being on fire, shall be dissolved, and the elements shall melt with fervent heat? Nevertheless we, according to his promise, look for new heavens and a new earth, in which dwelleth righteousness (2 Pet. 3:12–13).

THE PROMISE OF HIS COMING   8

This second epistle, beloved, I now write unto you, in both of which I stir up your pure minds by way of remembrance, That ye may be mindful of the words which were spoken before by the holy prophets, and of the commandment of us, the apostles of the Lord and Savior (3:1–2).

The fisherman-turned-apostle now switches from a scathing rebuke to a warm encouragement. Here he demonstrates the heart of a pastor for his beloved people. Again he admonishes believers to remember the fundamental tenets of the faith. We can sense the urgency in his desire to stir up their pure minds by way of remembrance. Perhaps we see in this the shadows of what he discussed in chapter 2. Indeed, his first words warn them of the scoffers who would come in the last days.

The English lexicographer Dr. Samuel Johnson once said that people more often need to be reminded than informed. Peter first plots a course down Memory Lane, preparing to share with believers the joy set before us in the riches of Christ. His pen etches the consummating propositions bound up in the Second Coming, God's irrevocable promise to keep His Word, His undying love toward dying men, and the eternal dimensions of a fading global order and a new beginning.

At the outset, Peter recalls his absolute commitment to the prime importance of a right relationship to the Word of God and again endorses as Scripture both the Old Testament and the New (the works of the apostles). The aged apostle knew well that the only antidote for error was found on the pages of the sacred writings.

His word to the early saints needs to echo in our ears in these last days. A trip to many Christian bookstores in America only confirms the desperate need for a revival of commitment to study the Bible. Reference sections containing commentaries on the Scriptures are giving way to books and materials that dwell on personal experience; interpersonal relationships; and ways to become healthy, well-adjusted "winners" in our contemporary culture. The situation is not an indictment of booksellers; they offer what their patrons demand. Yet Peter encourages a balanced system of study and exposition. We must never neglect the older Testament since it is, after all, the seed of the newer Testament. To explore seriously the Word, we must integrate the two, or we will never approach the heights of divine truth to which the Scriptures can take us. We neglect such study at our own peril.

SCOFFERS WHO ATTACK THE TRUTH

The first portion of chapter 3 revolves around Christ's Second Coming. Verses 3–9 contain essentially three movements: the scoffers who attack the truth, those who question the integrity of Christ, and the reason for the apparent delay in His return.

> *Knowing this first, that there shall come in the last days scoffers, walking after their own lusts, And saying, Where is the promise of his coming? For since the fathers fell asleep, all things continue as they were from the beginning of the creation (3:3–4).*

A basic concept arises here. It is the fundamental desire of unsaved people, religious or otherwise, to impugn the integrity of the Word of God. These scoffers are the same as those described in chapter 2. Their kindred spirits will appear in the last days and also will despise divine government, speak evil of God and angelic authorities, and boldly condemn matters they do not understand.

The root of their opposition to the very idea of the Second Coming is their own lust. Scoffers are consumed by lust. As far as they are concerned, they are the ultimate authority. No higher authority exists.

We find an example of this fact in the Old Testament book of Isaiah. The attitudes are the same, the issues are alike, and the outcome is predictable. Pro-Assyrian Jewish men controlled the religious authority in Jerusalem. Contrary to Isaiah, they were false teachers who were telling the people that it was sheer nonsense to believe destruction would come on Israel.

They said, "When the overflowing scourge shall pass through, it shall not come unto us" (Isa. 28:15).

In fact, however, these scoffers went on to claim, "We have made lies our refuge, and under falsehood have we hid ourselves" (Isa. 28:15). They had wrapped themselves in the fictitious security of a covenant with the enemy—but were in for a rude awakening.

They were guilty of telling people what they believed people wanted to hear; and they spread a false gospel of peace, plenty, and prosperity. Worse still, they lived under the delusion that they would continue to satisfy their lust at the expense of God's chosen ones. The scoffers' central problem was that they had pitted themselves against Jehovah and His Christ.

> *Therefore thus saith the Lord GOD, Behold, I lay in Zion for a foundation a stone, a tested stone, a precious cornerstone, a sure foundation; he that believeth shall not make haste* (Isa. 28:16).

The Messiah has been rightly referred to as a foundation stone and a costly cornerstone upon which the church is being built.

By contrast, the scoffers, false teachers, and their followers saw their alliance with the Assyrians annulled. They discovered, to their dismay, that the "hail shall sweep away the refuge of lies, and the waters [of judgment] shall overflow the hiding place" (Isa. 28:17).

> *Now, therefore, be ye not scoffers, lest your bands be made strong; for I have heard from the Lord GOD of hosts a destruction, even determined upon the whole earth* (Isa. 28:22).

History confirms that these ungodly types bit off more than they could chew (to use the vernacular) when they chose to pit themselves against Jehovah.

The Isaiah passage parallels Peter's warning and the content of chapter 3. Again we have a rather dramatic illustration of the fact that time does not alter the basic proclivities of willful sinners nor deter the Lord from His ultimate objectives. Sin is not a relative commodity that fluctuates with contemporary human attitudes. Absolutes do indeed exist in this universe. And though the world as we know it is moving toward destruction, a new creation is just over the horizon.

QUESTIONING THE INTEGRITY OF CHRIST

The rendering of verse 4 in the New International Version is illuminating and makes a strong point: "They will say, 'Where is this 'coming' he promised?'" Their central attack regarding Messiah's promise of a Second Coming is directed at the One who made the promise. It was Jesus who said He would come again. His statement on the subject was unequivocal:

> Let not your heart be troubled; ye believe in God, believe also in me. In my Father's house are many mansions; if it were not so, I would have told you. I go to prepare a place for you. And if I go and prepare a place for you, I will come again, and receive you unto myself, that where I am, there ye may be also (Jn. 14:1–3).

The promise relates directly to the Rapture of the church—His return for the saints. Jesus promised His sorrowing disciples that, one day, He will come to call believers to His side. And, forever thereafter, we shall dwell in His presence.

The catching-away of the saints referred to in John 14 is an imminent event. It can happen at any moment. And though some people labor diligently to deny it (as did first-century scoffers), there can be no serious question that first-century believers expected the Lord Jesus to come for them at any moment.

In Matthew's Gospel, Jesus made an equally unambiguous declaration. This time it concerned His coming with His saints to establish the Kingdom aspect of the Second Coming:

> *Immediately after the tribulation of those days*
> *shall the sun be darkened, and the moon shall not*
> *give its light, and the stars shall fall from heaven,*
> *and the powers of the heavens shall be shaken. And*
> *then shall appear the sign of the Son of man in*
> *heaven; and then shall all the tribes of the earth*
> *mourn, and they shall see the Son of man coming*
> *in the clouds of heaven with power and great glory*
> (Mt. 24:29–30).

Such adamant opposition to "the coming he promised" is not simply a difference of opinion about an eschatological point. These men Peter warns of despise the very idea of a Second Coming. Their temerity in assaulting the integrity of Christ is nothing new. The only difference between these false teachers and others is their extreme lack of subtlety.

In the heyday of higher criticism, certain "scholars" flatly denied or explained away virtually every aspect of miraculous activity recorded in the Scriptures. They also seemed to delight in questioning the authenticity of biblical sources. For example, they denied Moses' authorship of the Pentateuch. They argued that Moses did not write the first five books of the Bible, that they were written by a number of redactors who framed the content. Thus these books were not, as had been historically accepted, the books of Moses.

Their denial, however, went beyond the question of authorship. It attacked the credibility of Christ Himself. Following His resurrection, Jesus walked on the road to Emmaus with two crestfallen disciples. In the process of revealing Himself to them, the Bible says he began with Moses:

> *And beginning at Moses and all the prophets, he*
> *expounded unto them, in all the scriptures, the*
> *things concerning himself* (Lk. 24:27).

Jesus repeatedly referred to the words of Moses through-out the Gospel records. For example, in response to ques-tions raised by the Sadducees, He said,

> And as touching the dead, that they rise, have ye not
> read in the book of Moses how, in the bush, God spoke
> unto him, saying, I am the God of Abraham, and the
> God of Isaac, and the God of Jacob? (Mk. 12:26).

Jesus had no problem with Moses' authorship or author-ity. The higher critics were implying they knew more about the facts in the case than did Jesus. So the integrity of Christ was impugned. In their minds, the Lord Jesus Christ did not have an infallible grasp of truth.

Then arises the matter of Jonah and the fish. In the quest to debunk what they regarded as legends of the Bible, the higher critics went to great lengths to discredit the biblical account of Jonah. It was not possible, they pontificated, for the incident to be historical fact.

However, in speaking of His coming death and resurrec-tion, Jesus spoke of Jonah when He answered a group of scribes and Pharisees who had asked Him for a sign:

> For as Jonah was three days and three nights in
> the belly of the great fish, so shall the Son of man
> be three days and three nights in the heart of the
> earth (Mt. 12:40).

Jesus had no problem presenting the account as histori-cally accurate. The fact that He was speaking of His sacrifi-cial death and resurrection means that His critics were attacking a crucial element of His work on Earth. And, of course, they did not hesitate to do so. Why? Because their real problem was an utter lack of faith in the integrity of Christ, whom they were attempting to reduce to the level of an ordinary, error-prone human being.

The Second Coming is not something to be trivialized or dismissed as an inconsequential matter about which everyone has his own opinion. God cares what we believe about the coming revelation of the Messiah and what it will mean to us and the world about us. And it is a dreadful mistake for anyone to join the scoffers on this subject.

THE REASON FOR HIS APPARENT DELAY

For since the fathers fell asleep, all things continue as they were from the beginning of the creation (3:4).

Scoffers objected to the "coming He promised" out of a sense of unbelief rather than impatience. The continuation of all things since the fathers (Old Testament patriarchs) fell asleep was the proof they offered. They went even further, however, by contending that nothing had changed since the "beginning of creation." For them, the universe was a closed system operating on natural laws. Divine intervention by such a climactic event as the Second Coming was an absurd proposition. It follows that, if they believed this way about Christ's return, they did not believe the truth about His First Coming.

If all things continue as they were since the beginning of the creation, God could not have intervened with a supernatural event such as the virgin birth. Thus these false teachers/scoffers are again exposed as blatantly anti-Christ.

Their opposition to the return of the Messiah manifested their "faith." They were unbelievers who were pressing their own ideas, which ran counter to God's revelation. As is almost always true with false teachers, they fiddled the tune the masses wanted to hear; and their naïve followers considered their dogmatism and verbose rhetoric as legitimate skepticism. These false teachers were uncomfortable thinking about being severed from their ease in the here and now, much less the grim prospect of being personally accountable to God and facing His judgment. They were perfectly content to believe that nothing would or could ever change, and they were totally absorbed in the fiction of the permanence of the present.

We need to remember that Peter's warning related primarily to scoffers who would come in the "last days." Like their ancient counterparts, these people will sanctify their "faith" before their equally faithless brethren, employing pseudo-intellectual and simulated scientific jargon. The theory of evolution is an apt illustration.

Evolution cannot be verified scientifically. Yet much of contemporary education treats the theory as fact and ridicules anyone who dares to disagree. In reality, accepting the evolutionary hypothesis is a faith, not a scientific acquiescence to fact. The reason it has been so widely accepted is because it appeals to the minds of those who want to avoid divine dominion and the subsequent accountability it demands. Evolution is the brainchild of scoffers skilled in the art of giving people what they want to hear.

> *For this they willingly are ignorant of, that by the word of God the heavens were of old, and the earth standing out of the water and in the water, By which the world that then was, being overflowed with water, perished* (3:5–6).

All things have *not* continued as they were, and Peter counters that fallacious argument by pointing to the flood. Interestingly, he calls these scoffers "willingly" ignorant. They deliberately chose to ignore the fact of the universal flood. Their ignorance was self-imposed because they refused to accept the truth of the intervention of God and the consequent lessons of the catastrophe as recorded in Genesis. The flood taught that we live in a moral universe and sin will not go unpunished. Speaking of the last days, Jesus had something to say about the flood and the actualities associated with it:

For as in the days that were before the flood they were eating and drinking, marrying and giving in marriage, until the day that Noah entered into the ark, And knew not until the flood came, and took them all away, so shall also the coming of the Son of man be (Mt. 24:38–39).

The attitudes people had toward God's impending judgment in the preflood era were similar to those of the false teachers Peter spoke of. It was business as usual for them all because they had never personally experienced God's direct, divine intervention. They expected life to continue the same way forever. Their deliberate refusal to believe resulted in fatal consequences.

An unidentified schoolgirl of the 1940s said it well when she wrote, "Results are what you expect, and consequences are what you get." They felt that their attitudes and conduct would bring a satisfactory result. The consequences, however, were another matter.

By the Word of God, the world was created out of the watery chaos spoken of in Genesis 1:2:

And the earth was without form, and void; and darkness was upon the face of the deep. And the Spirit of God moved upon the face of the waters.

Two thoughts seem appropriate here. First, the world was formed from the brooding waters. Second, the earth would be sustained in the future by water benevolently provided by the Lord.

During Israel's great, festive national celebrations, offerings were brought in thanksgiving for the Lord's faithfulness in providing the annual early and latter rains. Withholding rain was often a way God chastised His people in times of national rebellion. The universal flood of Noah's day was a judgment on the whole of humanity, a fact that scoffers willfully deny.

Is it any wonder, therefore, that such strident objection has arisen in our day over the idea of a universal flood? It is one of the primary battlegrounds between evolutionists and creationists. For evolutionists, the very thought that a universal flood engulfed the earth is reprehensible. The root of their refusal to accept the obvious may well be their fear of being forced to acknowledge the possibility that an omniscient, omnipresent, and omnipotent God brought judgment by way of the all-engulfing waters.

But something else lurks here as well. Such people are at odds with the Father, yes; but they also deny the person and power of His Christ.

> God, who at sundry times and in diverse manners spoke in time past unto the fathers by the prophets, Hath in these last days spoken unto us by his Son, whom he hath appointed heir of all things, by whom also he made the worlds; Who, being the brightness of his glory, and the express image of his person, and upholding all things by the word of his power, when he had by himself purged our sins, sat down on the right hand of the Majesty on high (Heb. 1:1–3).

These verses emphasize a linkage between the creative and redemptive work of the Messiah. If you deny His power to create and control this universe, you imply that He is also powerless to redeem fallen men and women. Therefore, to deny categorically one aspect of Christ's person and work reflects negatively on the others.

> But the heavens and the earth which are now, by the same word are kept in store, reserved unto fire against the day of judgment and perdition of ungodly men (3:7).

Peter parallels the world that existed before the flood with today's physical universe and with what God has in store for it. Just as He created the antediluvian world out of the waters, He destroyed the living creatures of the earth by inundating that world with water. Now we learn that the postdiluvian world will be destroyed by fire. This concept totally defies comprehension by those who have embraced the fantasy that all things will continue as they have from the beginning of the creation. The same God who spoke the world into existence has reserved this present world for a fiery consummation.

The same thought appears in Malachi 4:1:

> For, behold, the day cometh, that shall burn like an oven, and all the proud, yea, and all that do wickedly, shall be stubble; and the day that cometh shall burn them up, saith the LORD of hosts, that it shall leave them neither root nor branch.

Malachi's reference is to the coming Day of the Lord, a subject the apostle will return to later in this chapter.

GOD IS NEVER LATE

> *But, beloved, be not ignorant of this one thing, that one day is with the Lord as a thousand years, and a thousand years as one day* (3:8).

Now, through Peter, the Lord begins to articulate the reason for delaying His return. First is the matter of the relativity of time. For us, a thousand years seems like an eternity. But to God, it is like a day. Consider the words of the psalmist: "For a thousand years in thy sight are but as yesterday when it is past, and as a watch in the night" (Ps. 90:4).

We can get a small inkling of this truth if we compare our attitudes as children with our attitudes as adults. As children it sometimes seemed as though a week was more like a month and a month, more like a year. For most of us, the interval between one Christmas and another seemed to last a lifetime. However, as we grew older, it was as though the clock sped up; and by the time we reached the end of a year, we wondered where the time had gone.

Those who suffer from self-imposed ignorance seem to be saying that, if God indeed promised to return at all, He was not in control of His faculties. Why would He make such an absurd promise if He did not intend to return in a reasonable amount of time?

Well, the Lord has an answer to their question. But it is one they were not then nor are they now prepared to accept:

> *The Lord is not slack concerning his promise, as some men count slackness, but is longsuffering toward us, not willing that any should perish, but that all should come to repentance* (3:9).

The good news is that the Lord is never late! And though there are times when we frail and impatient offspring of Adam and Eve are inclined to believe that He is, God is always right on time.

The story of Martha, Mary, and their brother Lazarus in John 11 illustrates this marvelous truth. Jesus was often a guest in their home. In fact, when He visited Jerusalem to attend Israel's great national feasts, He probably stayed with them. When Lazarus fell gravely ill, Mary and Martha sent for the Lord at once. After all, He had healed perfect strangers many times. Surely He would come immediately to minister to such a dear friend. However, when Jesus heard that Lazarus was sick, "he abode two days still in the same place where he was" (Jn. 11:6).

Not until Lazarus was confirmed dead did Jesus come to Bethany. Martha and Mary were beside themselves. Why hadn't He come when He was called? Was He indifferent to them in the single, greatest hour of their need?

When Jesus finally did appear, it seemed to them both that He was very late. And they did not hesitate to make their thoughts known: "Then said Martha unto Jesus, Lord, if thou hadst been here, my brother had not died" (Jn. 11:21). Mary later echoed Martha's words.

But these two women could not know that God was working beyond their field of vision. He soon called their beloved brother from the dark recesses of the tomb. And in so doing, He placed an irrefutable exclamation point behind His own soon-to-come resurrection from the grave.

Mary and Martha were involved in something wonderful and eternal in quality that would reach far beyond anything they could conceive. Yes, their Savior could have healed Lazarus before He had tasted death. But if He had done so, we would not have the marvelous evidence, 2,000 years later, of their brother having been raised from the dead.

God has a magnificent and practical word here for all of us. How many times have we, particularly amid personal trouble, questioned the Lord's timing? I'm sure you have heard deeply distressed believers say such things as, "Where is God when I need Him?"

We can rest assured that God is exactly where He should be, doing precisely what He should do. God is never late!

Now the Lord provides an explanation concerning why His coming has been delayed so long. It is a monumental revelation of the unfailing mercy of God.

A GRACE GIFT FOR HUMANITY

> But [God] is longsuffering toward us, not willing that any should perish, but that all should come to repentance (3:9).

We have been extended a magnificent gift of grace. First and foremost, people who are lost without Christ benefit from this delay. His long-suffering leaves the door of opportunity open for those who have not yet received Christ as their personal Savior. Although God's benevolence should not be considered an opportunity to delay the decision, it does reveal a patient and loving God who is dedicated to redeem rather than condemn. It is not His will that any should perish but that everyone should repent and find eternal life in Him.

It has been said, however, that no one will be in heaven who does not choose to go there. We must never assume that because God is merciful and long-suffering, He will excuse rebellion and unbelief and suspend forever the imposition of His divine justice. It is important we remember that He has also told us, "Behold, now is the accepted time; behold, now is the day of salvation" (2 Cor. 6:2).

We always hear a dramatic sense of urgency in biblical appeals to receive the gospel. Perhaps it is because we don't want our loved ones to find themselves among those who, too late, lament, "The harvest is past, the summer is ended, and we are not saved" (Jer. 8:20).

On the other hand, God has given a great grace gift to the church and a solemn rejoinder to all believers.

> *See, then, that ye walk circumspectly, not as fools but as wise, Redeeming the time, because the days are evil. Wherefore, be ye not unwise but understanding what the will of the Lord is* (Eph. 5:15–17).

We have just been told the will of the Lord: that people not perish but come to know life in Christ. The message rings loudly and clearly to a generation of Christians who, all too often, have become enamored with the here and now. The thought that we live in a world that is perishing has become increasingly repugnant to many professing evangelical Christians. Yet, if some of these self-absorbed believers find the subjects of death, judgment, and hell unsettling, it is never so with God. These facts must be faced. If we can come to realize how important it is to rededicate ourselves to the Great Commission and reach the lost, we can begin to understand what these truths mean to God's heart.

Outreach, however, will become progressively more difficult in the future. This world system is moving into a time of increased militancy against Christians who share their faith. I suppose we can liken it to the profound thought found in a simple, children's song that admonishes us to "dare to be a Daniel." Daniel entered a hostile environment when he was taken to Babylon. His captivity could have destroyed him spiritually. But rather than succumb to threats, intimidation, or the oppression of a hostile culture, he remained true to his faith and faithful to his mission.

We do not enter these last days with our eyes closed. It is incumbent that we know God's will and be quick to seize the moment for His glory.

Our generation has the greatest methodological and technological tools for evangelism ever known in the history of humanity. How tragic it will be if we squander these resources in the name of self-gratification.

CONCLUSION

It is good to remember that we have a promise. It comes from the One who personifies impeccable integrity and who has never failed to perform what He pledges.

Those whom God classifies in His Word as "scoffers" are not devoid of faith. They have a faith, but it is in their own particular beliefs, which they promote in opposition to those of us who believe in Jesus. In a sense, they are as much evangelists as those of us they ridicule. Their railings, denials, and opposition to the biblical faith in God, which we hold dear, should never intimidate us.

Perhaps the most comforting word for these last days is that God is never late. Indeed, our lives are in His hands, and we can rest in His perfect timing.

Of immeasurable wonder is the magnitude of the grace gift we have been given. We must never become complacent or careless by taking for granted the opportunities He has extended to us for now. We must move among lost men and women while the doors of opportunity are still open. When they close, it will be too late.

DAY OF THE LORD

9

But the day of the Lord will come as a thief in the night, in which the heavens shall pass away with a great noise, and the elements shall melt with fervent heat; the earth also, and the works that are in it, shall be burned up (3:10).

Throughout His Word, God admonishes believers to look ahead with a buoyant degree of optimism. We should be enthusiastic about where we are now and long with anticipation for what lies before us. Two thousand years ago, the church received a nonnegotiable commission. We were told to make Him known, in a balanced way, to all people until He returns—even to those in the farthest reaches of the earth. This command is not selective. The gospel is for *everyone*.

In reaching out to Jewish people with the message of the Messiah, we often hear, "To the Jew first." Although sincere Christians differ on how to interpret this part of Romans 1:16, one thing is certain: In the general scheme of evangelical pursuits, "to the Jew *first*" is never the issue. The issue is this one: Is it *to the Jew* at all?

Many programs for evangelism today are based more on market strategies than biblical directives. Such questions as "How do you get the biggest bang for the buck?" stem from this type of thinking. Unfortunately, return on investment does sometimes influence the decisions that church mission boards make. Consequently, those who are most resistant to the gospel, such as Muslims and Jewish people, are often relegated to the bottom of the appropriations barrel.

Their resistance to Christ, however, does not negate God's command to tell all people about Him. And, without a doubt, the single biggest thrill in the life of dedicated Christians comes when we are privileged to lead someone to the Lord and see a soul pass from death to life.

We look about us and see a fragmenting world. Political chaos, deterioration of planetary resources, a worrisome "hole" in the ozone layer, the potential of mass destruction, and too little space for too many people have all become part of the life experience. Where will it all end? This is the big issue now being addressed in many quarters. A serious desire exists to discover a suitable home for human beings somewhere other than on Earth. Interplanetary exploration has but one goal: finding another place to go. Space stations on the moon, Mars, or other exotic corners of the universe are being eyed as potential havens for humanity when scientists or bureaucrats eventually determine that our little orb has too many people or too few resources to support life as they know it.

However, as intellectually astute as modern man may fancy himself to be, the true solution to society's problems is not in outer space. Yet it is as old as the ages. God is still in control, and He has the plan. Scoffers may say what they will, but there shall be a "Day of the Lord." Peter sets before us the final thunderclap of the divine plan for this planet. By the time it is fully consummated, Satan will have had his way; man will have had his say; the Antichrist will have seen his day; and fallen angels will have gone their way. Then God will step in and write the last chapter—and what an awesome chapter it will be.

Bert Shadduck, writing in a slightly different vein in 1894, captured the finality of this divinely appointed stoppage of time in a hymn titled "I Dreamed That the Great Judgment Morning":

"From the throne came a bright shining angel,
And stood on the land and the sea,
And swore with his hand raised to heaven,
That time was no longer to be."

Earlier in chapter 3, the apostle warned the scoffers to remember that, before the flood of Noah's time, unbelievers were convinced all things would continue as they had in the past. People were marrying, giving in marriage, conducting business as usual, and expecting to do so for all the days to come. But they were wrong. Just beyond earshot, the waters of the deep were beginning to rumble.

In the rainbow that appeared after the flood, God placed a promise: Never again will He destroy the earth by water. However, a time will come when the planet will be consumed by fire. Ample warning has been given; it is mankind's responsibility to heed it.

Frankly, I have never quite understood why men never learn from history. They learn how to improve the toys and gadgets that make them more comfortable or wealthy. But the big issues—the ones that truly matter in life—they never seem to get a handle on.

On August 17, 1969, Hurricane Camille slammed into the Mississippi Gulf Coast with sustained winds of 190 miles per hour. Camille was the strongest hurricane in the United States since 1935.

The full ferocity of the storm was unleashed near Charlottesville, Virginia. Because the worst of the flooding came in the night, many people were not prepared to evacuate their homes. In one small area alone, nearly 100 people were swept to their deaths. For weeks to come, rescuers plumbed the bottoms of creeks, sifting through the huge piles of debris left by the storm, in search of bodies, many of which were never found.

As I drove through the area days later, I was amazed that, while some people were digging out the dead, others were busy cleaning the mud and rubble from the foundations of their former homes near the creek beds. They fully intended to rebuild on precisely the same foundations their residences had been swept from only hours earlier. We all know their justification: "It happened once. It will never happen again." Every time I ride through the area during a heavy rain, I wonder, "What are they thinking now?"

WHAT IS THE DAY OF THE LORD?

For many people, the Day of the Lord is restricted to the final, apocalyptic time related to the culminating judgments of the Tribulation period and the Second Advent of the Messiah. In fact, the Day of the Lord could well be referred to as the *Days* of the Lord because of the scope of events related to that time, as detailed in both the Old and New Testaments. The Day of the Lord covers a broad range of subjects, as Dr. John Walvoord explains:

> *Mentioned frequently in the Old Testament, the*
> *Day of the Lord refers to any special period where*
> *God intervenes supernaturally bringing judg-*
> *ment on the world.*[1]

An apt illustration of the biblical pattern for the events that compose the Day of the Lord can be seen in the universal flood. First there was the judgment of God. Then came the rainbow with its promise of better days.

Dr. Renald E. Showers addresses this twofold nature of the Day of the Lord in his book *Maranatha: Our Lord, Come!*

> *Thus, the Day of the Lord in the future will be at*
> *least twofold in nature. Just as each day of creation*
> *and the Jewish day consisted of two phases—a*
> *time of darkness ("evening") followed by a time of*
> *light ("day") [Gen. 1:4–6]—so the future Day of*
> *the Lord will consist of two phases, a period of*
> *darkness (judgment) followed by a period of light*
> *(divine rule and blessing).*[2]

Clearly, the Old Testament revelation establishes the validity of the twofold nature of this great event. It encompasses the *near* aspect of the Day in ancient times and the *far* view of what the Lord purposes to accomplish during the last days. In the future aspect, the darkness and light phases will stand in close proximity, as we shall learn.

THE DAY OF THE LORD THROUGH THE ELEMENTS

At times, particularly in the life of ancient Israel, the Day of the Lord involves specific judgments God sent through catastrophes of nature or intervention by foreign powers. In the book of Joel, God meted out judgment by intervening in nature:

Alas for the day! For the day of the LORD is at hand, and as a destruction from the Almighty shall it come. Is not the food cut off before our eyes, yea, joy and gladness from the house of our God? The beasts of the field cry also unto thee; for the rivers of waters are dried up, and the fire hath devoured the pastures of the wilderness (1:15–16, 20).

The question is, Why, during this Day of the Lord, were the rivers dried up and the food cut off? The answer is found in (1) the plague of the locusts that descended on rebellious Israel and (2) the devastating drought that accompanied it. The locusts are described as "a nation [that] is come up upon my land, strong, and without number, whose teeth are the teeth of a lion, and he hath the cheek teeth of a great lion" (Joel 1:6). A fierce companion of the "lion" was drought.

The only remedy open to the starving Israelites of that day was repentance. God called on the people and told them what to do:

Sanctify a fast, call a solemn assembly, gather the elders and all the inhabitants of the land into the house of the LORD, your God, and cry unto the LORD (Joel 1:14).

Severe judgment—locusts, drought, starvation—called for severe counter measures—fasting, prayer, and repentance. This supernatural intervention in Joel's day was designed to get Israel's attention and cause God's people to return to the pathway of His purpose for them. For the greater good of all generations that followed, it was imperative they did so.

The Day of the Lord and Foreign Armies

In Isaiah 13, we see the pattern of divine judgment and wrath as poured out on the Babylonians who afflicted Israel. The imagery here involves kingdoms, armies, and warfare; and both the near and future views of the Day of the Lord are evident. As relates to the near view, God says,

> *Wail; for the day of the Lord is at hand; it shall come as a destruction from the Almighty. Behold, I will stir up the Medes against them [Babylonians], who shall not regard silver; and as for gold, they shall not delight in it* (vv. 6, 17).

It is intriguing to observe how God orders events from His position of absolute sovereignty over both His people and the Gentile powers. He employed the Philistines, Assyrians, Babylonians, Seleucids, Romans, and a host of other nations to chasten Israel for its disobedience and rebellion. As incomprehensible as it may seem to us (and to the ancient Israelites, for that matter), God uses unbelievers to work His will for believers. A clear example of this fact is found in the first chapter of the book of Habakkuk:

> *Behold among the nations, and regard, and wonder marvelously; for I will work a work in your days, which ye will not believe, though it be told you. For, lo, I will raise up the Chaldeans [Babylonians], that bitter and hasty nation, which shall march through the breadth of the land, to possess the dwelling places that are not theirs. They are terrible and dreadful; their judgment and their dignity shall proceed from themselves* (vv. 5–7).

The Chaldean marauders exercised the desires of their hearts when they wielded their swords against Israel.

However, God visited retribution on them for their actions. The Bible intricately details the amazing downfall of Nebuchadnezzer's great empire. It bears repeating that those who take it on themselves to strike the Chosen People, in the end, will be stricken themselves.

THE LAST GREAT ACT

The event described in 2 Peter 3:10 is the final lash of divine judgment. It is the Day of the Lord in the fullest sense of the word—the moment of the final conflagration. In actuality, this phase brings us to the last event in the end-times scenario.

That event will occur at the close of the Millennium. The Rapture of the church, seven-year Tribulation period, judgment of the Gentile nations, Messiah's millennial reign, and the Great White Throne Judgment reserved for unbelievers will all be history. The long-anticipated day of the deliverance of creation will arrive at last.

> *For I reckon that the sufferings of this present time are not worthy to be compared with the glory which shall be revealed in us. For the earnest expectation of the creation waiteth for the manifestation of the sons of God. For the creation was made subject to vanity, not willingly but by reason of him who hath subjected the same in hope. Because the creation itself also shall be delivered from the bondage of corruption into the glorious liberty of the children of God. For we know that the whole creation groaneth and travaileth in pain together until now* (Rom. 8:18–22).

The final reclamation of the creation will take place when the heavens and earth as we have known them are destroyed. And that destruction will be spectacular. The dramatic language used to describe the event could just as easily describe the roar of thunder, the sound of flames, or the swish of an arrow sailing through the sky. Peter's terse, vivid expression "as a thief in the night" depicts swiftness and unleashed supernatural power. John Walvoord comments:

> *This will occur not at the beginning but at the end of the Day of the Lord which will be the end of the millennial kingdom...The description of the earth's being destroyed by fire is catastrophic and supports the conclusion that the new earth, created according to [Revelation 21] verse 1, will replace entirely our present earth. As scientists know, the earth is composed of atomic structure which is held together by the power of God. Just as God created it out of nothing, so He can dismiss it into nothing in preparation for the eternal state.*[3]

In one of Scripture's classic and calculated redundancies, Peter dispels all doubt about the totality of the coming devastation. This day of God will bring an event "in which the heavens, being on fire, shall be dissolved, and the elements shall melt with fervent heat" (3:12).

LIFE AND WITNESS

From the debris and ashes of the old creation riding the winds into the blackness of distant space, two exceedingly important propositions arise for the saints to ponder. Their essence can be captured in two words: *life* and *witness*.

> *Seeing, then, that all these things shall be dissolved, what manner of persons ought ye to be in all holy living and godliness* (3:11).

In the face of such overwhelming destruction of the material world, what should our attitudes be toward the present creation? If everything we see, touch, or possess is destined for the fire, how should we view it all? This question is particularly relevant for societies in the Western world. We are so saturated by affluence that we tend to regard the here and now as heaven and the heaven to come as something of only marginal and incidental importance. We may not want to admit it, but the signs are everywhere.

Russian-Christian philosopher Nicholai A. Berdyaev made a telling observation:

> We find the most terrible form of atheism, not in the militant and passionate struggle against the idea of God himself, but in the practical atheism of everyday living, in indifference and torpor. We often encounter these forms of atheism among those who are formally Christians.[4]

These are exceptionally strong words. Although Western cultures readily confess a form of belief in God, they exhibit a standard of practical atheism. They live as though God did not exist. Moreover, Berdyaev said, even many people who profess faith in Christ live, for all practical purposes, like pagans.

Peter denounces such behavior. The earth and all within it are only utilitarian instruments that God intends us to share and even enjoy, within proper proportions. However, He also intends us to remember our boundaries and the fact that we are simply tenants, not permanent inhabitants or landed gentry. The Bible calls us "pilgrims," even "strangers." We are sojourning on this earth for a season only. One day this ephemeral life will evaporate, and we shall go home to Him.

As a boy, I worked in a grocery store during the summer. One of my favorite chores was taking out and burning the boxes that supplies came in. Sometimes I stacked them neatly and thought of them as grand structures. Then I lit the match and consigned the boxes to the fire. They burned with great flames and fury. Then they were gone, reduced to ashes by a small boy with a match. Those "grand structures" were only flammable cardboard after all. Read Peter's words and then look around at the heavens above and the earth beneath. In the end, they are only cardboard; and God holds the match.

LIFE

The coming incineration of the visible universe and all of its concomitant tangibles reduces the reality of the material and elevates the value of human life—and how best to live ours. This is the intersection where the vagaries of the earthly touch the certainties of eternity. Indeed, here we learn that the true substance of life is the spiritual and eternal, not the temporal and time-shackled. Peter says we should be possessed with a desire to live holy and godly lives for Christ's sake.

Thus he brings us face to face with the absurdity of the common misconception that, while people come and go, the earth endures forever. The sun appears each morning; the moon comes up at night; the planet maintains its perpetual orbit; but men and women are born, only to die in the end. Such is the almost universal perception of existence. In this scenario, it is the world and its objects that are important. Men and women are incidental.

But the fact of the matter is that this concept is a reversal of reality. What we touch that is permanent in this life is people. People are important—not objects. One day our world will go up in a whirlwind of smoke and flame. People will endure for eternity.

In the final analysis, this is the truth that both Peter and Paul argued for most eloquently. Paul said he was willing to remain on Earth because the people he served still needed him. Peter makes the same point throughout his Epistle. He implores believers constantly to make their calling and election sure as he teaches and shepherds them.

Someone once said the consequences of the Day of the Lord lead to only three practical conclusions: (1) We should pursue holiness of life; (2) we should persevere in the worship of God; and (3) we should give ourselves to the service of man. Peter now turns to that last point.

WITNESS

> Looking for and hastening unto the coming of the day of God (3:12).

These words bring us face to face with a truth that is very nearly incomprehensible. The New International Version renders the phrase this way: "As you look forward to the day of God and speed its coming."

That believers could participate with the Lord in His eternal program in such a way as to hasten His return is a stunning revelation. Although He is sovereign in all of the affairs of time and eternity, He chooses to use us to help hasten the day of the final redemption. Such a stupendous thought should give believers everywhere a supreme sense of motivation. His coming and our association with it demand activity, not indolence.

This marvelous verse puts to rest a favorite theme of people who delight in ridiculing those of us who love the "blessed hope." We are not eccentrics who sit around wrapped in white sheets, huddled on the tops of mountains, with signs in our hands proclaiming "The End Is Near" as we listen for the trumpet to sound. The steady refrain of God's Word commands all who love His appearing to be busy serving Him with great effort and unflagging urgency.

How can we, as finite human beings, help hasten the day of Christ's return? Although we may not have all the answers, we know that He has already told us to live *holy* and *godly* lives and to share our faith. As Peter previously explained, the Lord seems to be delaying His coming because He "is long-suffering toward us, not willing that any should perish, but that all should come to repentance" (3:9).

Whatever else may be involved in hastening the day of God, one thing is certain—we are commanded to evangelize. And we must do so with every ounce of energy we have and every resource available to us. If we could choose one phrase that best summarizes the message of the entire Bible, it might well be *The Great Evangel*. God intervened in human history because the crowning achievement of His creation had fallen into sin and needed to be rescued. Thereafter, all the Old Testament ceremonies and sacrifices pointed to the day when the Perfect Sacrifice would appear. When He arrived, we discovered that God Himself had taken on the appearance of a man and had stepped into time in the person of His own Son, the Messiah.

For God so loved the world, that he gave his only begotten Son, that whosoever believeth in him should not perish, but have everlasting life. For God sent not his Son into the world to condemn the world, but that the world through him might be saved (Jn. 3:16–17).

John 3:16 is the fulcrum of the entire redemptive program. It is the sum total of why He has waited so long to effectuate reconciliation. We should not live like the scoffers, who impudently demonstrate their irritation with a God who patiently shepherds the ingathering of the wayward sons and daughters of Adam. We understand why He is waiting, we know what we must do in the interim, and we can rest in the fact that "our times are in His hands."

Although only He knows the day and hour of His return, we know there is a harvest to be reaped. And when the last sheaf is gathered in, He will call us from the field. A simple old song, long since cast aside by most of the saints of this generation, evinces our calling with heart and straightforward simplicity:

> "We'll work 'til Jesus comes
> We'll work 'til Jesus comes
> We'll work 'til Jesus comes
> Then we'll be gathered home."

CONCLUSION

God has given us inside information concerning the coming Day of the Lord, and it calls us to action. From this great wellspring of prophetic truth come practical elements concerning daily living. Peter teaches us what our focus should be regarding our personal lives, our relationships to other believers, and our burden for the lost all around us. Listen carefully and you will hear again the call to worship and revere Him who is the Alpha and Omega, the Beginning and the End, and everything in between.

A LOOK AT THAT 10
BETTER COUNTRY

Nevertheless we, according to his promise, look for new heavens and a new earth, in which dwelleth righteousness (3:13).

With these words, Peter ushers us through the gates of the heavenly city God promises to the children of light. It is the city our ancient, spiritual forebears longed to see. Though our view now is only through the eyes of faith, it is spectacular. Our assurance for eternity reposes in His promise of new heavens and a new Earth.

These all [Old Testament saints] died in faith, not having received the promises but having seen them afar off, and were persuaded of them, and embraced them, and confessed that they were strangers and pilgrims on the earth. But now they desire a better country, that is, an heavenly; wherefore, God is not ashamed to be called their God; for he hath prepared for them a city (Heb. 11:13, 16).

Earlier we saw the central divisions of the little Epistle of 2 Peter. We have looked at ourselves, examined the characteristics of our determined adversaries, and seen the Day of the Lord pass before us with great solemnity. Now we come to the grand consummation. All the dispensations, whether of law, grace, or the Kingdom with its splendor, are behind us; and we stand at the threshold of "forever after," the fulfillment of the age that will know no end—eternity.

ACCORDING TO HIS PROMISE

Both Old and New Testaments speak of this day. A marvelous example of God's promise from the Old Testament appears in Isaiah: "For, behold, I create new heavens and a new earth, and the former shall not be remembered, nor come into mind" (65:17).

In the New Testament, we have the words of our Lord:

> In my Father's house are many mansions; if it were not so, I would have told you. I go to prepare a place for you. And if I go and prepare a place for you, I will come again, and receive you unto myself, that where I am, there ye may be also (Jn. 14:2–3).

Peter concretely presents the Lord's promise regarding the eternal future of His people. He says we "look for new heavens and a new earth."

On the physical characteristics of the new heavens and new Earth, Dr. Walvoord had this to say:

> Further light is cast on the subject of whether the earth will be restored or destroyed at the time of the creation of the new heavens and earth. As Peter declared, 'That day will bring about the destruction of the heavens by fire, and the elements will melt in the heat' (v. 12). This description of atomic

*destruction of the earth leads to the conclusion
that the new earth will be entirely different with
none of the geographic landmarks that relate to
our present earth. There will be no more ocean, no
more Red Sea, no more Jordan River, no sun or
moon, the new earth will be entirely different as
described in Revelation 21—22.*[1]

THE NEW CREATION

What kind of place will this new Earth be? Men's attempts to describe such a grand vista universally have fallen far short of the coming reality. One individual, whose identity remains unknown, had this to say when asked what heaven would be like: "Well," he said, after reflecting for a moment, "I think heaven will be a place where the donkey finally catches up to the carrot."

His explanation, although somewhat prosaic, conveys the idea of satisfaction. Heaven will be a place where our souls will be completely satisfied. H. G. Wells's thoughts, in his *Outline of History* (Vol. 1), ring with a bit more profundity:

> *The doctrine of the Kingdom of Heaven, which
> was the main teaching of Jesus, is certainly one of
> the most revolutionary doctrines that ever stirred
> and changed human thought.*[2]

Flowing between these contrasting observations are volumes of human pontification with varying opinions on what the sum and substance of eternity is all about. For the earnest Christian, however, the only reliable source of information is the divine record of the Scriptures. Although God does not reveal every detail of the new creation, He tells us enough in Revelation 21 and 22 to whet our spiritual appetites. The apostle John's account begins where Peter's left off, with a chronicle of what will and will not be present on the new Earth:

> And I saw a new heaven and a new earth; for the
> first heaven and the first earth were passed away,
> and there was no more sea (Rev. 21:1).

It is a fundamental fact that there will be a literal and eternal new creation—the emphasis on *creation*. I am amazed to hear men teach of a heaven that will be less a reality than the earth we occupy now. A gossamer state of indefinite existence, lacking perceptible proportions or personal dimension, may appeal to the minds of the ethereally imprecise. The Bible, however, does much better by providing concrete facts about our future habitation:

> And he showed me a pure river of water of life,
> clear as crystal, proceeding out of the throne of
> God and of the Lamb. In the midst of the street of
> it, and on either side of the river, was there the tree
> of life, which bore twelve kinds of fruits, and yield-
> ed her fruit every month; and the leaves of the tree
> were for the healing of the nations. And there shall
> be no more curse, but the throne of God and of the
> Lamb shall be in it, and his servants shall serve
> him (Rev. 22:1–3).

And what do we say to this rendering of trees, streets, rivers, fruits, and nations? Is it, as some suppose, a lovely allegory to titillate our sin-stunted minds? It is nothing of the sort. If we do not fully understand all the elements, we should apply the same principles of interpretation we use with other portions of Scripture, that is, to accept the text literally, as God gives it to us. If any adjustments are needed, He is competent to make them for us. So what does He tell us?

ALL THINGS NEW

Four times in the first five verses of Revelation 21 we are told of new things. There will be a "new heaven" and a "new earth" (v. 1) as well as a new holy city, the "new Jerusalem" (v. 2). Plus God says, "Behold, I make all things new" (v. 5).

> *And I, John, saw the holy city, new Jerusalem, coming down from God out of heaven, prepared as a bride adorned for her husband* (Rev. 21:2).

This New Jerusalem is destined to be the eternal home of the saints of all ages. Today the Lord has placed a love for Jerusalem in the hearts of millions of His people. When the New Jerusalem descends from heaven, He will place His children in that city, which He has chosen for His name. But much more will be involved than is in the current dispensation of today:

> *And I heard a great voice out of heaven saying, Behold, the tabernacle of God is with men, and he will dwell with them, and they shall be his people, and God himself shall be with them, and be their God* (Rev. 21:3).

Scripture says, "We shall see him as he is" (1 Jn. 3:2); and we shall abide with Him forever. Tears, death, sorrow, crying, and pain will have no place in the celestial, holy city.

The richly embellished New Jerusalem defies adequate description. The Bible says the glory of God will illuminate it. And that glory will come from a very specific source:

And I saw no temple in it; for the Lord God Almighty and the Lamb are the temple of it. And the city had no need of the sun, neither of the moon, to shine in it; for the glory of God did light it, and the Lamb is the lamp of it (Rev. 21:22–23).

All Things Made Right

Peter places an addendum on his declaration in 3:13. Following the words *new heaven and new earth*, he adds, "in which dwelleth righteousness." These few words transport us to a realm we have longed for but never have experienced nor ever will while on this earth. In this greatest of all new worlds, sin will be unknown. In our polluted world, the great empires are depicted as marauding beasts, consuming one another and trampling weaker nations (Daniel 7). History has borne out the accuracy of Daniel's words.

The eternal state will have a social structure because the Bible teaches that kings and national entities will reside on the new Earth. Although God does not tell us the specific make-up or disposition of these nations, the Bible does say,

And the nations of them who are saved shall walk in the light of it, and the kings of the earth do bring their glory and honor into it [the new Jerusalem]. And there shall in no way enter into it anything that defileth, neither he that worketh abomination, or maketh a lie, but they who are written in the Lamb's book of life" (Rev. 21:24, 27).

People once sang of this land as (among other things) a place where we'll never grow old. They also intoned in melody the essence of the eternal reality when they sang "only glory, by and by." And so it will be. Gone will be sin and the desire to do wrong. Gone will be the heartache of sending our young to die in faraway places. No more wearying vigils beside sickbeds; no more weeping before open graves; no leaving home; no separation from other saints, particularly our loved ones who died in Christ. But best of all, we will live forever in the presence of God, never to be separated from Him. Only glory, by and by.

I once asked Israeli General Uzi Narkiss how he felt when he entered the Old City of Jerusalem during the Six-Day War in June 1967, after the Jewish people at long last retook the pearl and reclaimed the city of their fathers. He thought for a long while, then said, "I could say that I felt great, but it would not be enough." How could it ever be enough? He then said, "I will tell you, though, that at that moment, I felt that every Jew who ever lived was there beside me, caught up in such a cloud of joy."

How can we ever anticipate what it will be like to enter the New Jerusalem? We could say, "It will feel great," but it would never be enough. Indeed, how could a human tongue ever articulate the dimensions of what awaits us there?

> *And they shall see his face; and his name shall be in their foreheads. And there shall be no night there; and they need no lamp, neither light of the sun; for the Lord God giveth them light, and they shall reign forever and ever* (Rev. 22:4–5).

Only glory, by and by!

CONCLUSION

Two of the most persistent problems we face as believers today must be (1) discerning God's will and (2) regulating our priorities. Chapter 3 of Peter's Epistle can help us immeasurably in maintaining a healthy perspective toward God's will and putting first things first. Peter's divinely inspired words have exposed us to God's will for the heavens and the earth, as we know them. They will perish. Thus we must live on a higher plane, with a higher purpose, and not become seduced into developing strong attachments to the ephemeral things of the world that serve our present needs. A proper perspective simplifies our lives.

The first step in finding the will of God is to do the right thing right now. This attitude may appear overly simplistic, but it is not. When we practice doing the right things, day in and day out, everything else seems to fall into place. In the natural course of events, we find that opportunities for service begin to open, and in due time—God's time—we can settle into the area of ministry that the Lord has properly equipped us to fill.

We regulate our priorities by clearly evaluating what is *really* important in this life. With the world around us destined for destruction, what can be more important than people and the task of ministering to their needs?

Finally, no matter how dismal or difficult our circumstances or surroundings happen to be, we can live above them with the assurance that not only is a better day coming, but He is preparing a new creation. And, as we well know, we serve a God who does all things well.

GRACE TO   **11**
GROW BY

*Wherefore, beloved, seeing that ye
look for such things, be diligent that
ye may be found of him in peace,
without spot, and blameless (3:14).*

Peter admonishes believers to "look for such things" and
be diligent and alert for Christ's any-moment return. It
has been said that a person's relationship with Jesus
Christ is the first and last event in the journey through this
life. When we first become believers, our thinking is domi-
nated by the thought that we have "found the Lord." I
remember how full of meaning that little phrase was when
I first became a Christian. To hear of a friend or relative
who "found the Lord" was wonderful.

That emphasis marks the first stage of our journey. As we
approach the end of the journey, however, another thought
ascends to prominence. We wonder how God will "find"
(appraise) us. Peter again reminds his readers to watch for
the Lord's return and the new reality awaiting them.

Kenneth Wuest paraphrases 3:13 in an interesting way:
> *But new heavens and a new earth according to His
> promise we are looking for, in which righteousness
> is permanently at home.*[1]

Righteousness is a permanent resident in heaven and in those who will dwell there. The word itself expresses the essence of Peter's contrast between godless false teachers and true believers. In fact, it forms the line of demarcation between the charlatans, who repudiate righteousness in favor of earthbound and degenerate lifestyles, and true men and women of God. The unsaved are never at home with righteousness or truly righteous people. Therefore, they could never be at peace in the new creation, where righteousness is permanently "at home."

In stark contrast to their condition is that of true children of God who, having pursued blameless living in this life, will be found in Him in peace. God's children will have peace with fellow saints and peace in the new heaven and new earth.

As in 1:5, where Peter initially instructed us regarding the growth process, he urges believers to be diligent and work hard to develop a consistent Christian life and testimony.

Jude confirms Peter's admonition:

> *But ye, beloved, building up yourselves on your most holy faith, praying in the Holy Spirit, Keep yourselves in the love of God, looking for the mercy of our Lord Jesus Christ unto eternal life* (Jude 20–21).

THE PREDOMINANCE OF THE SCRIPTURES

> *And account that the long-suffering of our Lord is salvation, even as our beloved brother, Paul, also according to the wisdom given unto him hath written unto you; As also in all his epistles, speaking in them of these things, in which are some things hard to be understood, which they that are*

> *unlearned and unstable wrest, as they do also the other scriptures, unto their own destruction* (3:15–16).

Before wrapping up his Epistle, Peter speaks forcefully about the Lord's long-suffering as it relates to His delay in returning to Earth. His reference to long-suffering and salvation obviously looks back to verse 9 and God's unwillingness that any should perish but that all should come to repentance. People who make their stock in trade mocking the Lord's return attack the very core of God's love, mercy, and grace for errant humanity.

Peter is quick to appeal to the wisdom of his fellow apostle, Paul, who wrote along the same lines. The reference clearly puts to rest the idea that any animosity still lingered between the two after Paul rebuked Peter for his inconsistent conduct at Antioch (Gal. 2:11–14).

On the subject of Christ's long-suffering, Paul wrote,
> *Or despiseth thou the riches of his goodness and forbearance and long-suffering, not knowing that the goodness of God leadeth thee to repentance* (Rom. 2:4).

Peter also refers, in a general way, to Paul's teaching on long-suffering and repentance. In so doing, Peter said his beloved brother's Epistles contain other elements that are hard to understand and are regarded as ambiguous by people who are unlearned, short on interpretive stability, and quick to distort Paul's words. The idea here is that such people twist the text and impose a false interpretation—to their own destruction.

Examples of such distortions are found in various interpretations of Paul's teaching on justification by faith alone.

Some people claimed Paul taught that, once justified, believers were free to do as they pleased. Some went so far as to say that the more one sinned, the greater the exhibition of God's grace.

Another deliberate distortion of Paul's words concerns the Day of the Lord:

> *That ye be not soon shaken in mind, or be troubled, neither by spirit, nor by word, nor by letter as from us, as that the day of the Lord is present. Let no man deceive you by any means* (2 Th. 2:2–3).

Some of Paul's detractors claimed they had received divine revelation about the Day of the Lord and contended that the persecuted church had already entered that dark period. Someone apparently had forged a letter in Paul's name, making the same claim. Here again we see the extraordinary lengths to which false teachers will go to deceive people into believing they are true messengers of God. Peter calls these people "unlearned and unstable" and says they "wrest, as they do also the other scriptures, unto their own destruction" (3:16).

With those words, Peter sends us a resounding confirmation. The Epistles of the apostle Paul are Scripture—thus, the unadulterated, divinely inspired Word of the living God. Not only does he tell us that Paul's writings were inspired, but Peter places them on the same level as the Old Testament. No one can seriously dispute what the early church believed to be the Scriptures imparted by the Holy Spirit. Even at this early date, believers possessed written documents that confirmed what they had been taught in the Old Testament and provided instruction and guidance for their future. This fact alone makes deliberate false teaching even more despicable.

GRACE TO GROW BY

> *Ye therefore, beloved, seeing that ye know these things before, beware lest ye also, being led away with the error of the wicked, fall from your own steadfastness. But grow in grace, and in the knowledge of our Lord and Savior, Jesus Christ. To him be glory both now and forever* (3:17–18).

These final verses seem to encapsulate, by contrast, all that Peter presents in his Epistle. He first reminds his flock that they have been taught the truth—"seeing that ye know these things." They received ample warning about the great issues flashing between God's truth and Satan's fabrications. They knew what to believe.

He then warns them not to fall prey to the error of the wicked. Paul said much the same thing in Galatians in reference to his controversy with Peter and Barnabas:

> *For before certain men came from James, he [Peter] did eat with the Gentiles; but when they were come, he withdrew and separated himself, fearing them who were of the circumcision. And the other Jews dissembled in like manner with him, insomuch that Barnabas also was carried away with their hypocrisy* (2:12–13).

Barnabas, a man who should have known better, fell prey to error and was led from the path of truth. He was not steadfast in this matter. Peter says again, as he did in chapter 1, that if you grow and progress in the faith, you can be well equipped to live productively for the Lord. "If ye do these things, ye shall never fall."

Now we approach the crowning aspect of the Epistle. It sounds a purely positive note. Believers are to grow in grace and in the knowledge of the Lord. As we have seen, this growth is progressive. No Christian ever "arrives" in this lifetime. One of the great errors that beguile false teachers is pride in the belief that they are exceptions to this fact. They are certain they have arrived. Unfortunately, their confidence only assures their condemnation; they will never allow the truth to sway them from their error.

Yet, for all of their wisdom and knowledge, neither Peter nor Paul felt they had arrived at the pinnacle of perfection. A mountain still lay before them, and they pressed on. As Paul wrote,

> *Brethren, I count not myself to have apprehended; but this one thing I do, forgetting those things which are behind, and reaching forth unto those things which are before, I press toward the mark for the prize of the high calling of God in Christ Jesus* (Phil. 3:13–14).

The Word speaks of grace and knowledge. The Christian life does not begin with our physical birth. It begins with our spiritual birth through a personal relationship with Jesus Christ. Only by constant contact with Him, through His grace and knowledge, can Christian character and steadfastness develop.

Christians, like infants, are born to grow. To do otherwise is abnormal. We have available all the elements for nourishment; exercise; social and mental growth; Christ-esteem (as opposed to self-esteem, which the world considers so indispensable); and a clear, life mission. With these extraordinary gifts from God at our disposal, we arrive at the doxology:

> *To him be glory both now and forever. Amen.*

CONCLUSION

Never become bored with what you have learned from the Word of God. Many saints today complain that the preaching is shallow if they hear *just* a gospel message. Sometimes, I'm sorry to say, even veteran pastors, Bible teachers, and seminary professors can experience a functional indifference to themes they hear again and again. This may be one reason why new and sometimes bizarre teaching and interpretations seem more exciting than the "first things" Peter relied on to stir us up. The fundamentals of the faith are critical; and if they become as important to us as the air we breathe, we will stay faithful to the truth.

We also learn from this Epistle that those who handle the Scriptures must be bold and straightforward in correcting error. In the current Western culture, exposing false doctrine is not a popular thing to do. The "I'm okay, you're okay" syndrome has infected much of the evangelical community. Oddly enough, it appears that, although false teaching and rampaging evil increase, we hear little about what's truly wrong with society or how to correct it. Many of us long to hear the voices of the prophets thunder through the land.

Standing firm in these last days demands that we sustain an intimate relationship to the Word of our Lord Jesus Christ and our brethren dedicated to loving and serving Him. Corporate service for Christ must pulsate with evangelism, which reflects the heart of Him who is not willing that any should perish but that all should come to repentance.

Finally, our love for the blessed hope and our future home in the new creation should anchor every aspect of our lives. This world and all that is in it is passing away. But, like the Word of God itself, the things He is preparing for us will stand forever. And best of all, we shall stand with Him.

ENDNOTES

CHAPTER 5

[1] John Calvin, *Calvin's New Testament Commentaries: The Epistle of Paul the Apostle to the Hebrews and the First and Second Epistles of St. Peter*, William B. Johnston (transl.), David W. Torrance, Thomas F. Torrance (eds.), Wm. B. Eerdmans Publishing, Grand Rapids, Mich., 1979, p. 344.

CHAPTER 9

[1] John Walvoord, *Prophecy Knowledge Handbook*, Victor Books, Wheaton, Ill., 1990, p 486.

[2] Renald E. Showers, *Maranatha: Our Lord, Come!* The Friends of Israel Gospel Ministry, Inc., Bellmawr, N.J., 1995, p. 33.

[3] Walvoord, p. 512.

[4] Nicholai A. Berdyaev, *Truth and Revelation* (1953, repr. in *Christian Existentialism*, ch. 5, "Atheism," 1965), cited in *The Columbia Dictionary of Quotations*, Columbia University Press, © 1993, 1995; Microsoft Bookshelf '98 © 1987-1996 Microsoft Corp.

CHAPTER 10

[1] John Walvoord, *Prophecy Knowledge Handbook*, Victor Books, Wheaton, Ill., 1990, p. 512.

[2] H. G. Wells, *Outline of History*, Vol. 1, Ch. 28, Sct. 2, cited in *The Columbia Dictionary of Quotations*, Columbia University Press, © 1993, 1995; Microsoft Bookshelf '98 © 1987-1996 Microsoft Corp.

CHAPTER 11

[1] Kenneth S. Wuest, *The New Testament: An Expanded Translation*, Wm. B. Eerdmans Publshing, Grand Rapids, Mich., 1961, p. 513.

MORE BOOKS BY ELWOOD MCQUAID

THE ZION CONNECTON

Elwood McQuaid takes a thoughtful, sensitive look at relations between Jewish people and evangelical Christians, including the controversial issues of anti-Semitism, the rise of Islam, the right of Jewry to a homeland in the Middle East, and whether Christians should try to reach Jewish people with the gospel message—and how.
ISBN 0-915540-40-1, # B61, $9.95

COME, WALK WITH ME

From the award-winning "One Nation Under God" to the celebrated "Death Meets the Master," this inspiring assortment of poems, mini-biographies, delightful anecdotes, and devotionals will take you for a memorable stroll through time, through countrysides, and through the streets of Jerusalem.
ISBN 0-915540-47-9, # B37, $7.95

IT IS NO DREAM

Theodor Herzl, the father of Zionism, once said "If you will it, it is no dream." This amazing book scans the entire biblical prophetic program and shows how a faithful, promise-keeping God molded historical events to make the modern State of Israel a "dream come true."
ISBN 0-915540-21-5, # B02, $9.95

NOT TO THE STRONG

Journey to the time of the judges as Elwood McQuaid examines four "heroes of the faith" whom God chose to turn the tide and deliver Israel. Their frailties mirror our own—and what God did for them, He can do for us as well.
ISBN 0-915540-45-2, # B42, $8.95

ZVI: THE MIRACULOUS STORY OF TRIUMPH OVER THE HOLOCAUST

Millions of people have been touched, inspired, and encouraged by this story of a World War II waif in Warsaw, Poland, and how he made it to Israel and faith in the Messiah, to become God's man on the streets of Jerusalem. This bestseller will keep you spellbound as you live through the Holocaust with Zvi, then experience the history of modern Israel with this miracle man in a miracle land. It's a story you'll find difficult to lay down.
ISBN 0-915540-66-5, # B80, $11.95

Zvi's story is also available in Spanish in two separate volumes:

ZVI
ISBN 0-915540-62-2, # B01S, $8.95

ZVI Y LA GENERACION SIGUIENTE
ISBN 0-915540-63-0, B28S, $8.95

THE OUTPOURING

Enhance your understanding of how God certified the credentials of the Jewish Messiah among Abraham's seed in connection with the great, festive commemorations of the Jewish nation. John's Gospel will come alive as you discover the magnificant relationship between the feasts of Israel and the Lord Jesus Christ. *Also available in Russian.*

ISBN 0-915540-49-5, # B35 [ENGLISH], # B35R [RUSSIAN], $9.95

THERE IS HOPE

A Celebration of Scripture About the Rapture
What's ahead for the church? Learn how the church (1) is programmed for a sudden departure, (2) is going where death has no domain, (3) has no reason to fear the Antichrist, and (4) should look beyond His "Coming with Clouds."
ISBN 0-915540-21-5, #B02 *[ENGLISH]*, **$8.95**

Also available in Spanish by the title of **Hay Esperanza**.
ISBN 0-915540-64-9, #B02S *[SPANISH]*, **$8.95**